ESSENTIAL
PSYCHOLOGY
General Editor
Peter Herriot

B4

THE SOCIAL PSYCHOLOGY
OF ORGANIZATIONS

D1256674

ESSENTIAL

PSYCHOLOGY

THE SOCIAL PSYCHOLOGY OF ORGANIZATIONS

Frederick Glen

Methuen

First published 1975 by Methuen & Co Ltd
11 New Fetter Lane, London EC4P 4EE
© 1975 Frederick Glen
Printed in Great Britain by
Richard Clay (The Chaucer Press), Ltd
Bungay, Suffolk

ISBN (hardback) 0 416 84040 X
ISBN (paperback) 0 416 84050 7

We are grateful to Grant McIntyre of
Open Books Publishing Ltd
for assistance in the preparation of this series

Contents

Editor's Introduction

The way we spend our working life is largely dependent on the sort of organization we work for. Also, the experiences we have as children, as patients in hospitals, or as prisoners in prisons differ depending on the nature of the particular organization. Frederick Glen shows how the informal groupings in an organization may be very different from the formal ones; they may have norms of behaviour which sometimes conflict with the stated aims of the organization. Glen goes on to consider organizations as organisms which change as they interact with their environment, economic, political and social. He is able to show how conflict between individuals or groups may result either in disruption or in productive development.

The Social Psychology of Organizations belongs to Unit B of *Essential Psychology*. What unifies the books in this unit is the subject matter; all deal with social influences upon behaviour. Ranging from one-to-one interpersonal situations to the effects of organizational structures, all the writers are concerned with how the individual is affected by others or by the systems others have created. In order to cope adequately with their findings, they have had to develop different conceptual frameworks. The analogy of the human being as a computer (employed in Unit A) may

7

be appropriate, perhaps, to some one-to-one interpersonal situations. But to do justice to what happens in groups, new concepts (e.g. role) and new models (e.g. dynamic models) have been more useful. The reader will find other general conceptual frameworks in other units. They are not so much mutually contradictory as efforts to do justice to the complexity of psychology's subject matter. Living with a variety of explanatory frameworks decreases our confidence in psychology as a mature science, but perhaps it is better to be honest about what we don't know.

Essential Psychology as a whole is designed to reflect the changing structure and function of psychology. The authors are both academics and professionals, and their aim has been to introduce the most important concepts in their areas to beginning students. They have tried to do so clearly but have not attempted to conceal the fact that concepts that now appear central to their work may soon be peripheral. In other words, they have presented psychology as a developing set of views of man, not as a body of received truth. Readers are not intended to study the whole series in order to 'master the basics'. Rather, since different people may wish to use different theoretical frameworks for their own purposes, the series has been designed so that each title stands on its own. But it is possible that if the reader has read no psychology before, he will enjoy individual books more if he has read the introduction (A1, B1 etc) to the units to which they belong. Readers of the units concerned with applications of psychology (E, F) may benefit from reading all the introductions.

A word about references in the text to the work of other writers – e.g. 'Smith, 1974'. These occur where the author feels he must acknowledge by name an important concept or some crucial evidence. The book or article referred to will be listed in the References (which double as Name Index) at the back of the book. The reader is invited to consult these sources if he wishes to explore topics further.

We hope you enjoy psychology.

Peter Herriot

I
Introduction

A comprehensive definition of the processes involved in human behaviour would necessarily include, at one extreme, the minutiae of the psycho-physiological systems within the individual (see A2) and, at the other, the complex dynamics of relationships within and between the large groups that comprise society (see B5). The rapid growth of the behavioural and social sciences has led to successive sub-divisions of this massive area into fields of specialized study, such as we find in the titles of the *Essential Psychology* series. Each field has in varying degrees developed methods of study and analysis, models and theoretical constructs; many of them have produced further internal sub-divisions based upon divergencies in the theoretical orientations that emerge during their development.

It is not difficult to appreciate the necessity and the advantages of this pattern of development, but it is not without its dangers. In particular the student may tend to accept the sub-divisions as psychological fact rather than as methodological convenience, forgetting that the particular aspect of behaviour which he is studying cannot be a truly isolated or static phenomenon, but one that exists in a complete individual who is inevitably subject to a wide range of additional influences both internal and external, and who exists in a temporal context (see A1).

The student may even encounter some difficulty in finding a generally agreed definition of his area of study. Social psychology might be identified in terms of level of analysis as an area lying between the psychological study of the individual processes and the sociological study of large-scale societal processes. As a subject it is taught in both departments of psychology and sociology. Does the communality of interest between the two disciplines make this a meeting ground illuminated by two sets of complementary theoretical and methodological insights? Does the artificial division of the complex field of the behavioural and social sciences lead to territorial disputes making social psychology a battle-ground between conflicting factions? Or, perhaps, is it a separate area of study in its own right?

Even authoritative opinion seems to differ:

The details of social intercourse are the province of the social psychologist. This does not mean, of course, that no reference to social psychological matters will be found in sociological text books; they are there because the two disciplines overlap but they are not the main business of the sociologist.

... insofar as they [sociologists] are concerned with the details of interaction they are 'doing' social psychology, no matter what they call themselves.

It is, of course, a waste of time to quarrel about names, but one point is quite clear: the study of social interaction is one thing, the study of the framework of institutions and urban areas in which it takes place is another. (Sprott, 1958)

Sociologists, social psychologists and anthropologists have in general discovered the small group in working down from their traditional concern with macroscopic

10

social units. These students also tend to approach the study of the small group in terms of the traditional macroanalytic problems and general concepts. In the main, on the other hand, psychologists and psychotherapists have discovered the small social unit in working up from their traditional concern with personality. (Golembiewski, 1962)

Social psychologists study the problems arising for individuals from their membership of small social groups. Sociologists are concerned chiefly with the structuring and interlocking of social roles at work, in the family, the factory, the residential community and other bits of society. (Lupton, 1971)

If one were to accept some of the conceptual constraints implied by the above statements, it would be necessary to deal separately with the behaviour of people in an organizational context and with the social dynamics of the organizations themselves. In this introduction to the topic, however, it is felt that such a division is inherently unnatural. The behaviour of the individual is considerably influenced by group processes both informally and in organizational situations: the social processes of the organizations themselves are derived from the individual and group behaviour of the people who comprise them. It is important to examine the structure and dynamics of organizations, but it is people, not entities called organizations, who make rules, develop value systems, set goals and take decisions.

The individual in an organizational setting is much more than a basic unit of analysis: he brings with him his own complex internal environment derived from genetic inheritance and the totality of his past experience. In varying degrees he is influenced by the social pressures to which he is subject both within and outside the organization of which he is a part; and in turn he may, in varying degrees, facilitate or inhibit the activities of the organization. What

11

happens in an organization today is not solely determined by observable and immediate events; organizations, like people, have a history and are subject to both internal and external pressures, some of which are capable of being controlled and some of which are not.

It is sometimes tempting to simplify complex situations by imposing artificial and often arbitrary boundaries in the hope of producing more conveniently-sized areas of study. But such an approach often creates more problems than it solves. All too often the significance of an event can only be fully understood if we are aware of the total context in which it arises. For example, our domestic lives and our jobs are separable areas, but events in one can influence behaviour in the other.

In our approach to the social psychology of organizations, we may minimize some of the conventional barriers between areas of psychology or even between disciplines. After all, if a model derived from a source other than 'pure' social psychology seems relevant, why not examine it? It may not provide the answer but it could sometimes lead to a better understanding of the true complexity of the question.

2
The individual and the group

Even if we were to decide that the basic unit of analysis in social psychology should be the group, can we afford to ignore the role of the individual? We see ourselves as individuals – unique and complex entities with a variety of characteristics, some apparently fairly consistent and enduring, others which seem more transient, varying with the changing demands of our life situations (see D1 and D4).

At the same time, however, we are members of many groups (see B2), probably many more than we could list if asked to detail them. Some group memberships are determined for us at birth – sex, race, colour, family etc; some are chosen for us in childhood by our parents; some we decide upon deliberately – interest groups, clubs, societies, political parties; and some seem to arise by chance – friendship groups etc. In many situations, perhaps in the majority, our membership is determined by a number of interacting factors – personal, social, occupational, legal – so that it is often difficult to identify a single clear-cut reason for a particular group affiliation. In the case of interest groups we seem free to opt in or out of a group at will; in other situations we have little or no choice in the matter. If we wish to engage in a particular type of work, for example, membership of a trades union or of a professional association may be an absolute requirement.

Consider the possible group associations of John Smith, an imaginary but quite ordinary individual. John is thirty-two years old, born and brought up in Manchester. He was the second child in a family of three, his father was a tool-room fitter and an active trades unionist until his retirement, and has been a Methodist lay preacher for several years. John attended a local comprehensive school and served an engineering apprenticeship; he was a shop-steward before his promotion to foreman two years ago during a reorganization of the factory. Now he has been offered a post in the technical sales department of his firm. John's wife is ambitious and would like him to take the new job; they have two small children and have recently moved from a rented house near his parents and are buying a new house on an estate in the suburbs. John was a keen footballer and played for the firm's team but is now more concerned with training, spending most Sunday mornings at the sports' ground. His efforts there are generally appreciated, particularly by the chairman of the sports committee, who is the area sales manager.

The brief description of John Smith and his activities probably leaves out a great deal more than it includes. Nevertheless, the sketch indicates at least twenty areas of group association, influence, interaction and possible conflict which could be of importance in understanding his behaviour in a social context. Even in this simple case it can be seen that factors from past experience, immediate pressures and future aspirations could operate simultaneously as influences on behaviour, and that such influences could readily operate across the apparent boundaries between work, leisure and domestic life. Some of these group pressures call for closer examination.

Individual limitations in group behaviour

Certain physical characteristics of the individual will have an obvious effect in either facilitating or inhibiting his attachment to certain groups. This is particularly the case when the characteristic in question is obvious and permanent: a black skin will exclude you from a group that requires its members to be white – and vice versa; a police force with a minimum height requirement of 5 feet 6 inches will not employ you if you are 5 feet 2 inches; some occupations may be closed to you because of your sex. It is possible, of course, that the group may change its rules, so that those formerly excluded may be eligible for membership; but failing that, there is nothing that the individual can do in such cases to gain membership.

Other characteristics, while they do not constitute absolute barriers to group membership, reduce the probability of association. The requirements of the group may be realistic in relation to its activity or may be arbitrarily determined.

Individual differences in intelligence may also exert a limiting influence on group association. At the interpersonal level the relationship between intelligence, use of language and interests plays a part in the development of social ties. Although many groups exist in which a quite wide range of intellectual levels is present in the membership, they are generally based upon either a very specific common goal or a common interest capable of being held at various intellectual levels; many political and religious groups fall into this category. Groups whose activities make few intellectual demands may provide other forms of satisfaction for the more intelligent individual. Groups, on the other hand, in which participation requires a high level of intellectual activity are likely to be frustrating situations for those less intellectually endowed.

A further influence upon group affiliation, stemming

from differences in intelligence, is the effect of stratification in school classes, whether formal or informal in its initiation, and that of streaming within schools (see C4). Any system that tends to separate groups on the basis of intellectual level will tend to facilitate the growth of group ties at similar intellectual levels and inhibit others. This is not an argument for or against streaming in the primary school; regardless of whether or not steps are taken to separate children on the basis of intelligence, the nature of the educational system at secondary and tertiary levels is such that stratification will occur. In terms of our present discussion a major requirement for membership of groups engaged in higher education is the possession of a relatively high level of intelligence coupled with a successful exploitation of this resource in the earlier stages of an educational career.

There seems to be little reason to believe that comprehensive education will eliminate this process of differentiation. Different groups of pupils perceive different end-points in their educational careers and, as each group leaves the system, the links between them and the individuals who remain will tend to be broken or attenuated. This process has been evident for many years in Scottish grammar schools which functioned on a 'comprehensive' basis long before the term became fashionable. A and B streams followed a five- or six-year course, C, D and E streams a three-year course. Quite commonly, friendship groups might span several streams in the early secondary years, the tendency diminishing to some extent as interest groupings based on subjects and career intentions became more clearly defined. To a considerable degree group ties were broken when the C, D and E streams left; further separations occurred at the end of schooling when some pupils continued in tertiary education and others started work.

Clearly, intellectual level is not the sole determinant in

this situation but it must be seen as an important limiting factor, one of a number of interacting variables in a complex situation. In our later discussion we will see that the individual is simultaneously subject to the influences of several group allegiances, both formal and informal, operating within the organizational context of the educational or work situation.

If one asks the question to the effect: 'Why did you take part in that group activity?' most responses apart from the inevitable: 'Don't knows' would probably reflect that the individual gained some satisfaction from the experience, that he felt obliged to participate or that it enabled him to avoid some less satisfying situation. The question: 'Why didn't you take part?' might produce answers suggesting lack of interest, dislike, conflicting claims on time, some barrier to participation, etc. It is not intended to begin an examination of the psychology of motivation (see D2) but simply to suggest that, in most situations, the individual sees himself as able to exercise some degree of voluntary control over his behaviour. He feels that, in most situations, he can choose whether he participates or not. It is true that his intentions may have been determined to a considerable extent by past experiences of participation in similar situations, but he would probably argue that certain types of group activity are simply not his scene!

Without necessarily subscribing to any particular theory of personality we could reasonably expect to find certain consistencies in an individual's behaviour which might be termed personality characteristics (see D3). We are familiar with the extrovert who enjoys the society of his fellow men and would probably respond with enthusiasm if invited to a party; we also know the introvert who is happy with a quiet life and a good book, seems to find parties noisy and tiresome and would probably find an excuse not to come. We know too the dominant individual

17

who would seek out those group situations in which he could hope to play a leading part and the submissive individual who would be happy to follow but has no wish to lead.

In short, we might expect individual differences in personality to exert some influence on social behaviour – to facilitate or inhibit affiliation with different types of group situation. Similarly, personality differences may partly explain the divergences in the types of satisfaction found by different people in the same group situation (see D4).

Aspects of group structure

The significance of the family group as the first and probably the most important socializing experience which we encounter is discussed in detail elsewhere (C3).

Although variations occur from society to society in the constitution and extent of this primary group, its functions as a protective, supportive situation in which maturation and learning take place are crucial in the development of the individual, whether he is born into a primitive tribal group or a complex technological society (see C5).

A family is not, of course, an independent social unit. It exists as a group within an immediate social environment and in the contexts both of the accepted patterns of social behaviour of that local environment and of the general culture of the society of which it forms a part. It is not necessary to mount a complex sociological argument to make the case for the existence of sub-cultural groups within our own society; families in a West-country village, a council tower-block and the Surrey stockbroker belt could all be described as English, but the differences between them, both internally and in their social context, are clearly important.

Therefore, although we may talk about and examine similarities in the structure and dynamics of family groups, each remains a unique situation in the detail of its organization. The same comment applies to other groups and to organizations themselves; in comparing a light engineering factory on Tyneside with one of similar size and production in the London area, we will find similarities, but differences too.

It is within this basic group situation, the family, that the child first experiences the benefits and the constraints associated with group membership. Ideally the family provides the child with enough protection and security to enable him to develop as an individual; but, in practice, at one end of the range the family environment may provide insufficient guidance, consistency and support; at the other it may be rigid and over-protective. For better or worse the foundations of a child's attitudes in relation to authority and responsibility are determined by the learning experiences of his early years as a member of a family group. Elementary concepts of 'good' and 'bad', 'right' and 'wrong' are acquired long before the child is able to evaluate such concepts for himself, and reinforced by a system of reward and punishment which may be explicit or implicit in his parents' behaviour towards him (see B1). In this situation punishment need not be either physical or direct: to withdraw affection, to withold approval, to exclude from activities are effective punishments – not infrequently used by parents who claim that they would never punish a child.

Whether learned in the family group or not, the child soon becomes familiar with this type of sanction on his behaviour. He will encounter it in his first group experiences outside the family, in his relationships with other children. The behaviour that earns the approval or disapproval of the peer group may not be that which would produce similar reactions in parents, but the process is the same. 'Come and play with us', or 'We're not speaking to you' are potent influences on the behaviour of most children. The effects of acceptance or rejection by the group and the problems that arise from conflicting expectations in different group situations are important aspects of the child's social learning. He will meet them in more sophisticated forms throughout his adult life.

As the child extends the range of his group experiences the complexity of his social learning increases and consistencies begin to emerge in his relations with his fellows. In part, these consistencies represent an aspect of the emergent personality of the child; in part, the acquisition of the 'rules' or accepted conventions of social behaviour in his cultural milieu. Many personality theorists would point out that these two factors are far from being independent variables. For the purposes of our present discussion, however, it is the latter aspect that is of particular interest; it shows the formal learning of explicit rules in play and educational settings, and the informal acquisition of familiarity with differing behavioural expectations in a wide range of social situations. In either case, the ability to produce behaviour compatible with the expectations of the group is the essential qualification for acceptance (see B2).

The nature of society is such that external pressures upon the individual to conform – to fit in with the group – are central factors throughout the entire range of social experience. So general in fact, that 'normality' can be defined in terms of conformity with accepted norms of behaviour; failure to meet the criteria can earn for the individual at best a reputation for eccentricity, at worst a categorization of his behaviour as deviant or plain mad (see F8). In general, the pressures to conform are of two kinds: the fear of exclusion – of being seen as 'different' – and the rewards of security and support which follow acceptance. In the play situations of childhood and the controlled and contrived group situations of the classroom, we gain our first experiences of the results of success or failure in a social situation. We learn too that society will expect of the individual a sufficient degree of conformity to its norms and that there are penalties for failure as well as rewards for success.

To outline elementary social processes in this way is not to assume that each individual in a given situation will produce the same stereotyped reaction. The influence of individual differences cannot be ignored, nor can the variations in the rate and pattern of individual maturation. So, in similar situations of potential conflict between the individual and the group, one of us may be painfully aware of rejection by the group as an anxiety-provoking possibility; another, possibly less socially dependent or better endowed with self-confidence, sees the situation as a challenge; he may attempt to gain support for his view or try to find a group that more readily accommodates it. The extreme position of independence from group influences, the 'lone wolf', appears to be so rare that one might question its existence within the range of normal adjustment. By far the greatest number of those whose behaviour seems to deserve such a description are not isolated by choice, although they may have more or less successfully rationalized their position. The majority of children who remain isolated in group play situations watch from a distance but seem to fear the rejection of an approach to the group. A small number may remain in relative isolation because of psychological difficulties which have inhibited their capacity to form relationships with others. The truly isolated individual is the psychotic who cannot share in the group's perception of the world, nor they in his.

Formal concepts in group structure and dynamics

The topics of group structure and dynamics are complex, constituting developing areas within the body of psychological theory (see B2), but for our immediate purposes a

21

relatively limited form of description of group processes will serve.

As we have seen, we each belong to many groups and our memberships are determined by a variety of interacting influences. Some of our group attachments develop from chance meetings; some are imposed upon us by the nature of the society in which we live or by its formal legislation; some are sought because they seem likely to meet personal needs deeply rooted in our individual personalities. As we grow up and our group experiences increase in range and complexity, the interactions between personal character-istics and successive opportunities for social learning combine to develop attitudes and value systems. These will, in turn, play a large part in determining the forms of group membership that we would be likely to seek and those that we would tend to avoid. In differing group situations our awareness of membership may be character-ized by feelings of 'belonging', of support against external pressures, of obligation, of sharing in activities directed to-wards a common goal etc. In all such situations the be-haviour and attitudes of the individual members are in-fluenced to a greater or lesser degree by the group.

The part that an individual plays in the activities of the group of which he is a member may show considerable variation. From group to group his role relationships may differ; in one group his interactions with other members may be active and his contribution to the group's activities may be substantial; in another he may be a relatively passive member. He may hold high status in one group – leading, taking decisions, exercising control over others – but may be relatively low in the pecking order of some of his other groups. The role and status of a senior manager may be well-defined and high within his work organization but rather different as a new member of the golf club with a handicap of twenty-four.

Sherif and Sherif (1969) give clear and generally accept-

22

able definitions of the terms that will be used in this context:

> *A group* is a social unit consisting of a number of individuals who stand in role and status relationship to one another, stabilized in some degree at the time, and who possess a set of values and norms of their own regulating their behaviour, at least in matters of consequence to the group. (p. 131)

> *Role relations* refer to patterns of reciprocal behaviour and associated expectations between two or more individuals that are characteristic and recurrent in interaction of consequence to them. (p. 140)

> *Status* is a member's position (rank) in a hierarchy of power relations in a social unit (group or system) as measured by the relative effectiveness of initiative (a) to control interaction, decision-making and activities, and (b) to apply sanctions in cases of non-participation and non-compliance. (p. 140)

> *A social norm* is an evaluative scale (e.g. yard-stick) designating an acceptable latitude and an objectionable latitude for behaviour, activity, events, beliefs, or any other object of concern to members of a social unit. (p. 141)

Different types of group have been described; the commonest simple categorizations would include the *primary group* – a small group in which all the members have frequent face-to-face contact – as opposed to a *secondary group* – one which is formally set up, impersonal and in which the contact between members is less frequent. The members may be widely dispersed and, in some cases, may not even constitute a group in the psychological sense of the term.

Again reference is often made to the *informal group* – one that arises spontaneously as in the case of friendship groups – as opposed to the *formal group* – where at least some aspects of its structure, goals and role relationships are predetermined and where the norms of group behaviour are often explicitly stated and formally enforced with the support of specific sanctions, e.g. work groups, professional societies etc.

The categories of formal and informal groups, however, are often found in the same situation, as any formally-constituted group of people will tend to develop informal relationships and groupings within it in the course of its normal day-to-day activities. We may, therefore, expect to find informal groups within any formal structure. This aspect of group behaviour is of some importance and will be examined at greater length in the following chapter.

Reference groups
Kelvin (1969) traces the evolution of this term from its first use in the limited sense of groups within which the individual compares himself in evaluating his status to the more general sense in which the term is employed today. In particular, he emphasizes the distinction between groups of which the individual is a member, where the norms of the group can impose compliance with particular standards or behavioural expectations, and those groups of which he is not a member. In the latter case, compliance and identification depend upon a voluntary acceptance of the standards and values of the group.

The adoption of the norms of a group of which the individual is not a member is of particular significance when a change of role is required. His perception of the norms of the new group serves as a model in terms of which he can develop the new forms of behaviour which will facilitate his acceptance as a group member. This process is sometimes formalized in training situations; the officer cadet in training and the mechanic on a supervisors course both learn something of the norms and expected patterns of behaviour in the groups which they aspire to join, in addition to the formal skills and procedures in-

24

volved in the new role.

A similar process occurs as a more informal change of values in individuals who aspire to upward social mobility. In an unpublished study of a new council housing estate, marked differences were found between the attitudes and values of families who saw their move to new council housing as an end goal and those who saw it as a step towards the eventual goal of home ownership. The latter tended to adopt the attitudes and values of their contemporaries in a nearby private estate, often suffering a certain amount of conflict in the process. Their less aspiring neighbours referred to them as 'the would-be nobs'.

The formation and modification of attitudes

Attitude was defined by Allport (1935) as:

> A mental and neural state of readiness, organized through experience, exerting a directive or dynamic influence upon the individual's responses to all objects or situations with which it is related. (p. 810)

Many variations and developments in the definition of attitude have been produced during the succeeding forty years, but the majority belong to this general class of description (see B3).

> An attitude is an organized and consistent manner of thinking, feeling and reacting with regard to people, groups, social issues, or, more generally, any event in one's environment. Its essential components are thoughts and beliefs, feelings (or emotions) and tendencies to react. (Lambert and Lambert, 1964: 50)

Or, rather more briefly: 'Put quite simply, any attitude towards an object is a compound of what I know or believe about it, how I feel and what I am inclined to do about it.' (Kelvin, 1970: 41)

25

It is not our present purpose to review the extensive literature on the nature, development and measurement of attitudes. In addition to the companion volumes in this series the reader is referred to texts such as Sherif and Sherif (1969) and Kelvin (1970) and to collections of readings such as Fishbein (1967) and Insko (1967).

Studies of organizational behaviour may employ measures of attitude in a variety of ways; as indicators of work adjustment, of actual or potential reaction to change, and of areas of tension within and between the groups of which the organization is composed. Some examples of such studies are given in later chapters.

Two brief reminders might be offered at this point: first that the concept of attitude is an important link between the individual, interpersonal and group levels of behavioural analysis; second, that the influence of attitudes upon behaviour need not be an entirely conscious process. The latter point implies that the statements of even the most co-operative individual about his attitudes in a particular context may well be incomplete. As Oppenheim (1968) observes:

> People are often poor predictors of their own behavior, so that statements of intent often lack validity when compared with subsequent events, though they may well have been valid as statements of hopes, wishes and aspirations. (p. 73)

The stereotype has frequently been described and discussed as if it was a form of ideational malfunction with associated undesirable characteristics of bias and prejudice. It is important to appreciate that the process involved in stereotyping is rather more general than this view would suggest, based on the tendency to use a form of categorization as part of our perceptual processes (see B2, A4). The complexity of the patterns of attitudes, values and behaviours in the groups which make up our social environment – both those with which we are directly involved and those which we only hear about – is such that no-one could give a completely accurate, factual description of the characteristics of all the groups of which he is aware. Nevertheless, we attempt to structure the world around us in terms of the best-fitting total interpretation of each set of partial information that is available to us.

One way of attempting to make our social environment more systematic and predictable is to create categories that enable us to perceive complex issues in a simplified form. The problem arises from the component character-istics of such categories being not only over-simplified but also, in varying degrees, inaccurate. For example, if I had no contact with university students and based my view of them as a group upon random items in the popular press, I could hold the opinion (or develop the stereotype) that students are lazy, untidy individuals, given to smoking marihuana, and mainly interested in revolutionary activi-ties, free love, and how best to live off the taxes paid by honest, hard-working members of the community. A less stereotyped view of the student group based upon actual contact would have to qualify the simple picture con-siderably: the greater the experience with the group con-cerned, the less likely it would be that any general stereo-type would emerge.

Following Kelvin (1970) it would seem that this form of over-generalization on the basis of inadequate or in-accurate information leads to the use of stereotypes in which we attribute norms to groups within our environ-ment and consequently expect certain attitudes and values to be characteristic of members of such groups.

It follows that, if my view of a group is based upon a stereotype, the accuracy of my initial judgements and the effectiveness of my communication in actual contact with a member of the group may be reduced. By definition, stereotypes relate to groups; contact with actual individuals

27

is likely to provide evidence less than completely compatible with the stereotype. If the stereotype is well established, however, the individual case which does not fit is likely to be rationalized as an exception to the general rule.

Prejudice is a phenomenon closely associated with stereotyping; in some respects it could be regarded as an extreme example of this phenomenon. Most of the research carried out in this field, and many of the definitions of the term, deal only with the negative aspect of prejudice (e.g. Sherif and Sherif, 1969:268). In view of the fact that imbalance of judgement as a result of favourable prejudice can be as important in many situations as the negative form, it is worth including both aspects in any definition.

Essentially, prejudice is an attitude, usually with an emotional loading, either hostile or favourable to actions, objects, persons or doctrines of a particular type, to the extent that the individual will tend to prejudge any issue in the area concerned. While stereotyping appears to be a general source of over-simplification and possible bias in social judgements, prejudice is a more specific phenomenon and can cause substantial distortion of judgement. There is evidence that prejudice arises more frequently in association with rigid, over-controlled types of personality adjustment, e.g. the authoritarian personality (Adorno *et al*, 1950).

Modification of attitudes

The history of attempts at changing attitudes is certainly a good deal longer than the history of social psychology, arising, most probably, from the realization that if an individual could not be coerced to behave in a particular way, he might be persuaded to do so. In the course of history efforts have been made to persuade people to support one cause rather than another, to buy in one shop rather than in another, to follow a particular faith or vote for a particular party. These all show signs of recognition, perhaps unconscious, of both the cognitive and affective components of attitudes and also of doubts as to the relationship between apparent changes of opinion and actual changes in behaviour.

The present century has produced an impressive range of research studies in the laboratory and in the field, as well as numerous practical exercises directed at attitude change at every level from individual to national (see B3). Some examples of methods which have been used are outlined below, not in an attempt to summarize this complex area, but simply by way of illustration.

The presentation of new information is unlikely to be sufficient in itself to produce modification, as a well-established attitude can exercise a screening effect in such situations. We are more likely to attend to and accept information compatible with our existing attitudes than that which is discrepant. The approach immediately raises the question of the credibility and authority of the source of the information. Asch (1952) presented to his subjects a quotation from Jefferson expressing sympathy with 'rebellion'. Subjects told the true author of the quotation interpreted this term as 'agitation'; those told that it came from Lenin interpreted it as 'revolution'.

In another experiment, after initial attitudes towards juvenile delinquency had been established, subjects were presented with a recorded talk advocating a lenient approach to the delinquent. Attitude change was greatest in the group who believed that the speaker was a juvenile court judge, less in the group who were told that the talk was by a randomly chosen individual, and least in the group to whom the speaker was presented as a drug-pedlar. The actual message was identical in each case (Hovland and Weiss, 1951).

However, as Sherif and Sherif point out in reviewing social-psychological research in attitude change:

The one-way flow model of influence does not embody the typical case in modern life.... Even in the laboratory (not to speak of the classroom or neighborhood), the very properties of the source (his trustworthiness, competence, expertise and credibility) depend upon his relationship to the reference sets or reference groups in which the person participates, or his standing therein. (1969:473)

The importance of group influence upon attitude change was well illustrated in studies comparing the effect upon attitudes of information presented in the form of a lecture with that found when the groups were able to discuss the issue in question (Lewin, 1965). The potency of the influence of groups in modifying attitudes is emphasized in the follow-up of Newcomb's well-known field studies at Bennington College in the late 1930s (Newcomb *et al*, 1967). The liberal ethos of the college was shown to have produced significant and persistent change in a range of initially conservative attitudes with which the girls entered the situation. The degree of change was greatest in those who had found stable roles within the informal group system and was further related to the length of time spent in the community.

In addition to the method used, factors related to the attitudes themselves must also be taken into account in any consideration of attitude change. Such factors are classified under seven general headings by Krech *et al* (1962).

1. *The extremeness of the attitude*. Although, in general terms, difficulty in changing an attitude is directly related to its extremeness, the relationship is perhaps more complex than at first appears. Extreme positive and extreme negative attitudes present particular problems; the possibility arises here that the problem is one of modifying prejudice, with its associated high affective loading.

2. *Multiplexity*. The breadth of the attitude or the number of component elements must be considered. Attitudes in relation to broad concepts, such as 'management' or 'trades unions' are likely to be composites with some internal variation in attitudes towards particular examples or particular activities of the general class.

3. *Consistency*. This is seen as the balance and coherence of the cognitive and affective components and the behavioural predispositions associated with the attitude. It is suggested that attitudes that present some degree of inconsistency between these elements will be more susceptible to change.

4. *Interconnectedness*. An attitude that is widely related to other attitudes which tend to support it is likely to be resistant to change.

5. *Consonance of the attitude cluster*. This category is related to the preceding one but emphasizes the degree of interrelatedness and cohesion of the constellation of attitudes involved. An attitude that is part of such a mutually reinforcing system will be more difficult to change.

6. *The number and strength of the needs which are served by the attitude*. The suggestion here is that the more closely the attitude is related to important elements of the motivational processes of the individual, the more difficult it will be to change.

7. *Centrality of related values*. This aspect refers to the extent to which an attitude is associated with the fundamental personality characteristics of the individual. Where change in an attitude would require a fundamental alteration of personality it is likely that any modification of the attitude would be particularly difficult.

The above summary is a reminder that an attitude is unlikely to be a discrete, independent unit or a readily separable aspect of the individual concerned. More probably it is part of a complex, interrelated set of attitudes and further related to other aspects of individual adjustment.

Any adequate model of attitude change must cover the full range of processes involved, which may be seen as falling into three general stages.

1. *Preparation for change.* Normally change will not be sought for its own sake nor will the individual be ready to respond to a demand for change unless he perceives the need to do so as more pressing than the reasons for resisting it. The initial approach to the problem must include the presentation of the change situation in such a way as to reduce the perceived level of threat and, ideally, to motivate positively the individual to accept the change.

2. *The process of change.* Given that the need for change and its direction have been accepted, the individual is faced with the task of learning new attitudes. The process may involve learning through identification with influential individuals or groups who hold the attitudes in question; it may involve the adoption of the new attitudes through the discovery of their instrumentality in dealing with situations and problems. The probability that the new attitudes will be internalized is increased if their effectiveness is demonstrably greater than that of the attitudes previously held. Rokeach (1968) distinguishes between two aspects of attitudes in any given situation; these are attitudes in relation to objects and attitudes in relation to situations. To concentrate attention upon changing the object attitude might leave the situational aspect unchanged. This type of result has been observed in training situations where a significant change in the object attitude, e.g. the benefits of job enrichment, could be demonstrated after training;

however, the situational attitude towards maintaining a set level of production was unchanged, with the result that no change of behaviour in the actual work situation occurred (see E3).

3. *The consolidation of change.* It is necessary that the changed attitude should not only lead to new patterns of behaviour but that the cognitive, affective and behavioural components should be sufficiently well integrated into the personality and behaviour patterns of the individual to ensure the permanence of the change. If the consolidation of the new learning is incomplete, there is a possibility that the new pattern will break down and the old one will re-emerge. An office manager had been trained in a new control system which required both different work patterns and different attitudes towards staff. He completed the training and appeared to work well for a time under supervision. When left to work independently, however, problems arose which were beyond his capacity to resolve. The new learning broke down and he reverted to the former work patterns and to the associated attitudes.

3
Organization: structures, authority and power

In one sense, we all know about organizations – we have had first-hand experience of them certainly from the day we first went to school. We buy goods in them, work in them, live in towns and cities administered through them and in a country governed through them. It does not follow that we are always aware of our involvement or that we understand fully the part which they play in our lives. Sometimes we welcome them as safe, supportive structures; sometimes we fear or blame them as the sources of constraints and impositions upon the individual; but, inevitably, in a complex society we are to a considerable extent dependent upon them.

Schein offers a definition which clearly identifies their major characteristics:

> An organization is the rational co-ordination of the activities of a number of people for the achievement of some common explicit purpose or goal, through division of labour and function, and through a hierarchy of authority and responsibility. (1965:8)

As soon as one conceives of a desired purpose or goal which is beyond the capacity of one man to achieve, some

34

form of co-operative activity is necessary. Such co-operation may or may not be voluntary but, in either case, there is a need to state clearly what the purpose or goal of the activity may be, to identify and define the steps by which the goal is to be reached and to decide what the individual contribution to the process should be. Such decision is necessary whether it is imposed by a dictator or arrived at by consensus – the differences in this decision process are clearly of importance to the organization. Any complex organizational activity requires a division of labour and specialization of function and, in order to ensure that the several contributions are appropriate in form and content and are made in the desired sequence, some form of control must be exercised. Different systems of control can be employed but they must provide direction, information, instruction, to ensure that the subsidiary goals of the contributing parts of the organization are achieved in the correct form, time and place, to produce the desired total outcome.

This complex pattern of relationships, although dependent upon people for its existence and activities, has continuity as a total unit. Its structure has a high degree of stability, although individuals may enter or leave the organization or move to different positions within it. Although it is tempting, and sometimes convenient, to think of an organization as having individual organismic identity, it can be dangerous to carry this tendency to the point of anthropomorphism by attributing the human processes which take place within it to the organization itself. In this situation one is liable to displace personal responsibility for actions and events by blaming 'the system', 'the rules', 'higher authority' (unspecified), rather than examining the psychological and social factors involved. As has been suggested, the structure of an organization imposes constraints upon the behaviour of its members, limiting freedom of action and choice in a variety of situations; it does not, however, prescribe every form of behaviour which takes place within it.

Power and authority

The concept of power or authority has been employed as a basis for the classification of different types of organization. Etzioni (1964) offers a classification comprising three fundamental types: the predominantly *coercive* form of authority, based upon the use of compulsion, which would be represented by concentration camps, prisons, custodial hospital institutions etc; the predominantly *utilitarian* where control is exercised through a form of rational-legal authority and is supported by a system of economic reward, such as we find in business and industry, the government service, trade associations and peacetime armed forces; the predominantly *normative* in which involvement is based upon the intrinsic value of the activities performed or of membership itself, examples of which would be found in religious or ideologically-based organizations, voluntary bodies and professional organizations. Etzioni also includes hospitals and universities in this category. Mixed forms are also identifiable – normative-coercive, utilitarian-normative and utilitarian-coercive.

The system is extended to specify the expected forms of involvement of members in the classes of organization described.

Alienative involvement, in which the member is obliged to remain with the organization and has no psychological commitment, would be expected to occur most frequently within a coercive authority structure.

Calculative involvement, characterized by a reasonable return for services rendered in membership, would be most typical of utilitarian structures.

Moral involvement, in which the work is performed

basically because it is valued and where psychological commitment to membership is present, would be the most usual form of involvement under normative authority.

Although few organizations would be found on examination to be pure examples of such categories, the characteristics are readily recognizable and serve to identify important classes of structural constraint which influence the nature of members' involvement with the organization. Some aspects of current negotiations and dispute situations in the universities and in the hospital service have shown differences in the attitudes of members of the same organization which would suggest, in terms of the above typology, that calculative and moral forms of involvement are present. This can present a conflict situation for the people concerned, represented both in the individual changes in the nature of their involvement and also in a clash between group loyalty and personal value systems, e.g. when professional associations first consider the use of industrial sanctions, such as the work-to-rule and the strike.

Weber (1946) makes a distinction in his writings between power and authority which is of some importance (see B5). Power is exercised when one individual is in a position to exercise his will in a situation – to carry out his wishes regardless of resistance from others involved in the relationship. Authority, in this context, implies voluntary compliance with demands that are essentially perceived as legitimate. Although this system applies most directly at the level of total societies, it has been used in describing organizational systems of smaller scale. Three types of authority are distinguished:

1. *Traditional*. In this case authority is granted to the ruler on the basis of his inviolable, pre-determined right to that position, as in the 'divine right of kings'. Formal acknowledgement of superiority is made to the ruler and, in so far

as he has delegated authority, to other senior members of the hierarchy. This pattern may be found occasionally in old-established family firms in which control is accepted as passing from generation to generation. To a lesser degree the need to defer to traditional authority is found in many organizations.

2. *Charismatic.* Here authority derives from the influential personality of an inspired, visionary leader, often seen as possessing extraordinary, even supernatural powers and likely to gather a following of disciples. The phenomenon occurs most frequently in religious and political movements. This type of authority frequently takes a revolutionary form, rejecting traditional values, though later tending to become 'routinized' in order to maintain its function. In organizational settings leaders can arise who gain support and acceptance in this way, largely through the influence of personal qualities.

3. *Rational-legal.* Here authority is based primarily upon belief in the supremacy of law and the acceptance of rational criteria for its assignation. A position of authority in this context is earned by ability, expertise and acceptance of the rules and procedures that govern the system.

This is seen as the basis of the concept of democracy and of formal organizations.

Bases of power

French and Raven (1959) in their examination of the nature of power in a social context identified five forms of power which could constitute bases of leadership:

1. *Reward power.* There will be a tendency to comply with the requirements of those who are seen as being able to give or withhold reward. Such reward may be in a con-

crete form, but there are many other ways in which this form of power can be exercised.

2. *Coercive power.* Essentially the power to punish non-compliance. A form of power of doubtful value in most organizational settings in that it represents a last resort. If punishment is not effective, what then? For this reason officer cadets in the services were at one time instructed never to give an order if they knew it was likely to be disobeyed!

3. *Expert power.* This is exercised by the individual who possesses knowledge, skill or expertise which is in demand in that context.

4. *Referent power.* The individual who is popular with his fellows and admired by them exercises power within his group.

5. *Legitimate power.* The position which the individual holds within the organizational structure confers power over those who are subordinate to him.

Bureaucracy

The concept of bureaucracy, as described by Max Weber (1946), has exercised considerable influence upon the sociological approach to the study of organizations (see B5). It is important to emphasize two points which bear upon the current use of the term:
1. Weber described an idealized type of organization – a structure which would maximize administrative efficiency. This description was not based upon the analysis of actual organizations; it was a theoretical model which has served as a starting point for research designed to test the hypothesis implicit in his descriptions of the administrative

process. The original statement, however, is hypothetical rather than factual and it is not always easy to distinguish between statements that are derived from systematically tested hypotheses and those that are impressionistic elaborations of the basic model.

2. Blau and Scott (1968) distinguished between the colloquial use of the term 'bureaucracy' – 'rule-encumbered inefficiency' – and the sociological usage as being neutral, referring simply to the administrative aspects of organizations. There has however been an increasing tendency for the word 'bureaucratic' to become an emotionally-toned term or to carry ideological overtones. It might be suggested that views employing this usage, however interesting, should be treated with caution.

The five essential characteristics of a bureaucracy identified in Weber's description of 'modern officialdom' may be summarized as follows:

1. The activities necessary for the support of the bureaucratic structure and the associated areas of authority are officially defined, distributed as duties and supported by a stable structure of rules. Only those appropriately qualified and formally authorized to exercise control are employed; the requisite qualifications and methods of control are also governed by rules.

2. All bureaucratic structures possess different levels of authority in a graded hierarchical order, regulating the super- and sub-ordinate relationships of their component parts. Such an arrangement is found in all bureaucratic structures whether public or private.

3. The uniformity of operation is ensured by management procedures based upon written documents. Associated activities and forms of behaviour are determined by regulations.

4. The nature of contacts between officials and between an official and the public are similarly governed by the rules pertaining to his office and his position within the hier-

archy. Contacts are therefore impersonal and the distance between hierarchical levels tends to be maintained.

5. The holding of a bureaucratic office is more than a job – it is a vocation. Formal training and qualifications are essential requirements for entry and the future life of the official is bound up with a complex system of obligations and associated rewards. He owes loyalty to an impersonal or functional purpose rather than to any individual.

The ease with which one can recognize many of Weber's observations in our own experiences of dealing with officialdom makes it easy to forget that what is described is an idealized, hypothetical structure. Real organizations, however, are composed of people and human behaviour cannot be limited by the artificial constraints of a theoretical model.

In Chapter 4 we will consider some of the problems arising from the fact that variations in individual, interpersonal and group behaviour must inevitably complicate any organizational system.

Clearly, in spite of differing formulations, some of the above typologies and models are identifying similar classes of phenomenon. Although they are described under the general heading of organizational processes, it is possible to identify within them characteristics stemming severally from the structural, group and individual aspects of the situation. Analyses that attempt to restrict themselves to a single level inevitably fail to consider some relevant variables in that power and authority are exercised by individuals upon other individuals or groups. Almost invariably this occurs within some form of organizational structure.

Organizational classification in terms of benefits

A further form of organizational classification is offered by Blau and Scott (1968) in terms of who receives benefit from the existence of the organization. This typology is suggested on the basis of the argument that in order to survive, any organization must perform some kind of useful function. Should it fail to do so, it no longer fulfils the basic reason for its existence.

Blau and Scott identify four types of organization:

1. Mutual-benefit organizations, in which those who benefit are the actual members of the organization: e.g. trades unions, professional associations, religious and political groups, social clubs etc.

2. Business organizations, which exist primarily for the benefit of their owners, managers, share-holders: e.g. industry, commerce, banking etc.

3. Service organizations, in which the main beneficiaries are the clients: e.g. educational institutions, hospitals, social services etc.

4. Commonweal organizations, from which society as a whole derives benefit: e.g. government departments, local authorities, police, fire services etc.

From the above outline it might be considered that, with the exception of the first category of mutual-benefit organizations, the question of benefit to the members of the organization itself is incidental. It is possible, however, that change in the internal dynamics of an organization could alter its nature in terms of this classification; such possibilities are foreshadowed in the increasing interest of the employees of business organizations in profit-sharing schemes and in worker participation in management. The classification remains stable only so long as the relationship between the organization and its members is satisfactory, economically and psychologically. Any system within which the members of an organization cannot be actually compelled to participate in its activities must take account of the needs, expectations, aspirations and attitudes of its members if it is to continue to function adequately.

The extensive literature in this field has been reviewed by Pugh (1966), identifying the main groups of theorists as management, structural, group, technology and economic. In *Writers on Organizations* some of the major contributions in the development of the field are described (Pugh *et al*, 1971).

Scientific management

In the development of organizational theories we find these primarily concerned with prescriptive systems, on the bases of which they say how organizations ought to be managed – emphasizing the *how* rather than the *why* aspects of the manager's task. In the case of industrial management such views trace their origins to Taylor's concept of the machine theory of organizations and the 'scientific management' school in general (Taylor, 1911) (see E1 and E5). In administration, the writings of Fayol (1949) and Urwick (1947) have been influential. Such theories show little interest in the individual or group processes and, particularly in the case of the exponents of 'Taylorism', saw the worker as another resource to be exploited.

> Now one of the very first requirements for a man who is fit to handle pig iron ... is that he shall be so stupid and so phlegmatic that he more nearly resembles ... the ox than any other type ... he must consequently be trained by a man more intelligent than himself. (Taylor, 1911: 59)

> To manage is to forecast and plan, to organize, to command, to co-ordinate and to control. (Fayol, 1949:5)

> I am convinced that a logical scheme of organization, a structure based on principles, which take priority over personalities, is in the long run far better both for the morale of an undertaking as a whole and for the happi-

ness of individuals, than the attempt to build one's organization round persons. (Urwick, 1947:31)*

In general, the basis of such systems was first to design the job then to fit the worker to it. It is important to remember, however, that although thinking on management during the first quarter of the present century seems to have been dominated by the scientific management approach, not all the theorists of the day saw this as simple resource exploitation.

Still more important than the valued commercial profit on both sides is the cultural gain which will come to the total economic life of the nation, as soon as everyone can be brought to the place where his best energies may be unfolded and his greatest personal satisfaction secured. The economic experimental psychology offers no more inspiring idea than this adjustment of work and psyche by which mental dis-satisfaction with the work, mental depression and discouragement, may be replaced in our social community by overflowing joy and perfect inner harmony. (Munsterberg, 1913:309)

Pugh points out that few of the prescriptions of management theorists have been closely scrutinized and that they do not appear always to work in practice.

As Woodward points out:

The danger lies in the tendency to teach the principles of administration as if they were scientific laws, when they

* Convictions can change, however; ten years later Urwick expressed his view in the following terms: 'any business ... can be looked at from two levels. It is –

1. An organization of economic values for an economic purpose.
2. A community of human beings, joined together for common as well as individual purposes, in other words a social unit.

Personally, I believe that ability to look at a business from this second level, to realize it as a social unit, is fundamental ... And the group undoubtedly has a personality of its own ... we spend much of our time ... considering individuals and their impact upon the group and the group and its influence upon individuals.' (Urwick, 1957:8) are really little more than administrative expedients found to work well in certain circumstances but never tested in any systematic way. (1965:128)

The Human Relations movement

The work of Elton Mayo and the significance of the Hawthorne investigations is referred to elsewhere in this series (E5) and described in detail by Roethlisberger and Dickson (1939). Originally envisaged as a one-year study of relations between conditions of work and the incidence of fatigue and monotony among employees, the studies extended year by year as it became evident that the influential variables at work were psychological and social rather than physical. New research methodologies were developed to deal with new problems; the indirect approach in interviewing replaced the direct approach; concepts of leadership were re-evaluated and attention was drawn to the importance of communication as an area of research. Perhaps most important was the realization that an appreciation of informal organization was essential to the understanding of shop-floor behaviour.

Kelly (1969) gives a summary of the findings of the Human Relations school in which he emphasizes the importance of the realization that social and psychological motives could be more influential than economic ones in structuring the behaviour of workers. The conflict between the personality of the individual and the demands of the work situation is clearly stated and it is suggested that such individual needs cannot be fully satisfied in an organizational context.

From this source, too, stems the mass of research during the 1930s and 1940s exploring the complexities of the informal group structure of organizations and their associated systems of roles, relationships, norms and sanctions. Related to this was the examination of the supervisory role, in particular the differing effects of task-centred and

45

employee-centred supervision.

In the studies of the primary work group, attention was drawn to the so-called restrictive practices syndrome as one of the fundamental manifestations of the workers' response to the demands placed upon them by the organization. Conflict at the management level was also examined: line versus staff friction illustrating the competing demands of different goals within the management structure and differing definitions of goals within the sub-systems of the organization.

Simon (1955) reviewed studies supporting several of the original Hawthorne observations:

1. the very act of observing or investigating worker behaviour can influence the behaviour studies and produce changes in attitudes – *the Hawthorne effect*;

2. the opportunity for interaction between employees in the work situation tends to increase both morale and productivity and lack of interaction reduces those effects – *the interaction hypothesis*;

3. change in the behaviour of a group is produced more rapidly and effectively when the people concerned in the desired change participate in deciding what its nature should be and how it might best be achieved – *the participation hypothesis*;

4. as people respond strongly to the attitudes and value systems of groups with which they have frequent face-to-face contact, an individual who has close contact with two or more groups which hold conflicting attitudes and values tends to find himself in a situation of personal conflict – *the cross-pressures phenomenon*.

The contributions of the Human Relations group have been both valuable and influential but, in a sense, the movement was a pendulum swing away from the rigours and strictures of the thinking of scientific management. In recent years there has been a tendency for the pendulum to swing back towards the centre, not in the rejection of human relations as an important area, but in a more critical view of the extent to which its contributions meet the demands of current work on organizational behaviour.

Kelly (1969) suggests that there was a tendency to build upon inadequate theoretical foundations, generalizing from particular observations to a possibly excessive degree. The concentration upon the individual/group level of analysis is also felt to be limiting. The complexities of organizational structure and the socio-economic context of the organization itself may not be taken sufficiently into account.

There has been a further source of criticism in the suggestion that, although the pendulum swing as a reaction to the 'economic-man' model of scientific management was a reaction in the right direction, the movement was too extreme. This is implicit in the view that, while job satisfaction is an essential element in the understanding of the work situation, it is not the sole purpose of work. Nor is the shop-floor the only appropriate area of study; the problems of management cannot be fully explored on a human relations basis. Different organizational structures and different organizational goals generate a variety of problems which call for forms of analysis beyond that of the primary work group. Similarly, these factors impose different constraints upon the individuals concerned and suggest that there is no perfect theory or ideal prescription applicable to all levels of organizational analysis.

Organizational influences upon the individual

Forehand and Gilmer (1964) discuss a number of ways in which the organizational environment acts upon its members so as to produce differences in their behaviour. In particular they identify three groups of influences:

1. *Definition of stimuli*. Particular stimuli which act upon the individual in his work situation may be determined by

a range of environmental factors, both external and internal. The demand for a particular product, the economic climate, the state of the labour market may influence management practices and, in turn, the conditions of work. Within the organization itself structural characteristics or current management philosophies will also act upon the individual to facilitate or to inhibit different patterns of behaviour, e.g. an engineering company formerly specializing in large one-off units built to order introduced a new product involving batch production. Although account had been taken of the need to train workers in new procedures and to introduce appropriate technical and control systems, the ramifications of the change had been underestimated. It took several months for the workers to adapt to the structural changes in the organization and to the different demands of the work situation. Former practices – and to some extent skills – were effectively devalued and new forms of behaviour and attitudes to work were expected.

2. *Constraints upon freedom.* The structure of an organization may limit or prevent certain types of behaviour. Management may be affected by restriction of freedom of comunication or of autonomy; e.g. a manager of a branch factory had been required to present monthly reports to a consultative group at the parent factory and to seek approval of minor modifications to production schedules. During reorganization it was noted that in no instance during a period of eighteen months had this consultation resulted in any need to modify the branch manager's original intention. The abandonment of the practice saved time and money and enhanced the satisfaction of the branch manager and his team.

It was found, in another case, that in a new branch factory recently built and commissioned at a cost of

£8½ million, the centralized purchasing and wages system of the parent organization led to a situation in which the only actual cash available to the branch factory manager was a £5 petty cash float.

3. *Reward and punishment*. The organization can also determine, quite apart from the formal payment system, ways in which particular forms of behaviour are reinforced. In one situation a particular action might be praised as a constructive exercise of initiative; in a more rigid setting the same action might be criticized as exceeding the authority of the individual concerned.

The psychological contract

A further aspect of factors that influence the behaviour of the individual in an organizational context is seen in the concept of the 'psychological contract' described in the work of Argyris (1960). It is to the effect that the reciprocal expectation of the individual and the organization extend well beyond any formal contract of employment governing the work to be done and the reward to be received. Although there is no formal agreement, there will be an understanding between them that a wide range of customary practices, rights, privileges and obligations will be honoured and observed by both parties. This psychological contract is an important element of any work relationship involving aspects of the situation that can be important determinants of behaviour.

We have mainly concentrated in this chapter on the structural theories which are seen as concerned primarily with the form of organizations, their co-ordination of function and task allocation in relation to the achievement of their goals. Factors such as size, location, technology etc. produce their characteristic structural differences.

4
Formal and informal processes in organizations

Structural descriptions

As soon as a task reaches a level of complexity such that more than one person is needed to carry it out, we are faced with the two problems which are primary concerns of organization theory – division of work and the differentiation of responsibility and authority. These are the essential components of the definition of an organization which we adopted in the preceding chapter and we find them as the basic components of any description of organizational activity, from the day-to-day activities of primitive peoples to the most sophisticated activities of modern civilization.

Perhaps the commonest representation of the structure of an enterprise is the organization chart (Fig. 4.1). This represents the way in which the component units of an organization are arranged and shows the various forms of division and specialization of function. The immediate value of this method of presentation is to show the general shape of a complex structure in a readily comprehensible form. In its commonest form it also shows the hierarchical

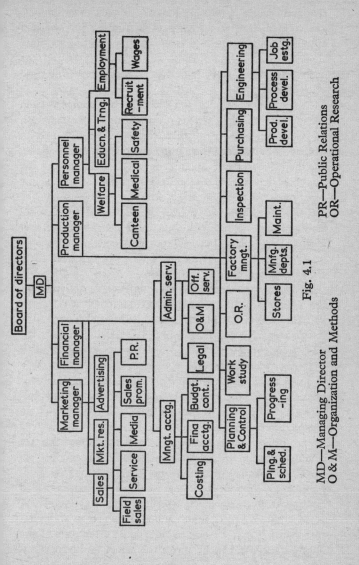

Fig. 4.1

MD—Managing Director
O&M—Organization and Methods
PR—Public Relations
OR—Operational Research

51

structure which is typical of most complex organizations, the vertical dimension representing the several levels of authority within the structure and the connecting lines showing the relationships between these levels and the channels by which communication takes place within the organization.

In spite of superficial similarities between organization charts, no two organizations are the same. It is important to remember that even when the same title is used to describe a particular function in two organizations, not only are there likely to be differences in the definitions of the title but the vertical and horizontal relationships of the functional positions in the two companies will not be identical. We will consider later the additional complexities arising from the fact that functional titles represent not idealized occupants but real people whose activities and relationships are by no means confined to those stated in the job specification.

As part of the process of co-ordination of activities for the achievement of a goal, decisions must be taken. As the vast majority of organizations are hierarchical in structure, the pattern of authority-responsibility relationships is the most frequent determinant of decision processes; it is often prescribed that a particular class of decision must be taken at a particular level within the organization. Such decisions often represent the exercise of one or other type of power (see Ch. 3) vested in the individual by his position within the hierarchy. This exercise of authority may be perceived as a positive phenomenon, recognizing an appropriate differentiation of specialization or seniority; it may be perceived as negative in that it unreasonably limits the freedom of the subordinate, under-values his competence and detracts from his satisfaction in his work situation. There is no simple rule of thumb method by which an authoritative decision may be classed as 'good' or 'bad', or, more appropriately, as beneficial or detrimental to the functioning of the total organization or the achievement of a particular goal.

Some situations lend themselves more readily than others to different forms of decision-taking. A planning decision which determines the future development of an organization would, in almost every case, benefit from the widest possible range of contribution from those who are concerned in the outcome of decision or who can contribute from a basis of relevant expert knowledge or experience. If an immediate decision or action is to be taken, however, it is not difficult to envisage a situation in which an immediate authoritative decision which is 70 per cent correct is to be preferred to a delayed consultative decision 90 per cent correct but too late to be effective.

It might even be considered that the patient on the operating table would generally prefer the decision on the site of the incision to be made by the operating surgeon, however authoritarian, than by the democratic decision process of everyone in the operating theatre.

Generally, democratic decision processes are rare phenomena in an organizational context; when they do occur they most often operate within certain organizational constraints or are subject to a gradual formalization through time. As we have seen, a complex task calls for division of labour and allocation of authority and reponsibility. Starting from a fully democratic position of everyone having a voice in decisions, both student representative groups and workers' co-operatives tend towards a situation in which particular duties are allocated to groups or individuals and appropriate authority is delegated to them by the group as a whole.

Likert (1967) identifies four systems of management which illustrate some of the problems with which we are currently concerned.

System 1. Decisions are generally taken at the top of the

53

organization, management is authoritative and exploitive, distance between superiors and subordinates is considerable and clearly defined, communication is typically downwards and the compliance of subordinates is gained by coercion.

System 2. Major decisions are taken at the top although some minor ones may be delegated, management remains authoritative but benevolent, tending to use rewards rather than threats to obtain compliance; attitudes towards superiors tend to be subservient and communication upwards usually passes only what the superior wishes to hear.

System 3. Although general policy decisions are taken at the top, more specific decisions are delegated to lower levels and some consultation is encouraged so that subordinates have some influence upon their work situation; reward is used more frequently than threats but communication upwards of unwelcome information is still cautious and limited.

System 4. Decision-making is widely dispersed throughout the organization, management encourages group participation and involvement in setting goals and determining methods, using economic rewards; communication upwards and downwards is free and accurate and barriers between superiors and subordinates are psychologically less rigid. The process of group decision-making involves overlapping groups within the organization; the individuals who form the bridge between groups are described by Likert as 'linking pins'.

Although Likert regards System 4 as the most generally effective form of management, he points out that other forms can be technically efficient even if psychologically stressful. He sees the appropriate management style as being determined by the particular conditions of each situation and by the relationships between the people involved in them. General principles can serve as a guide, but the demands of each management situation possess unique aspects calling for careful examination and sensitive judgement.

It has been suggested that a crucial factor in the management process and organizational dynamic is the nature of the actual work situation and the technology involved. Woodward (1965) studied production systems in order of increasing complexity, relating these to differences in the organizational structure and system of control, later producing a typology based upon the classification of control as personal/impersonal and uniting/fragmented (1970). In personal control the processes of planning and execution are closely associated; the extreme case would be that of the owner/manager who is directly involved in decisions regarding costs, standards, production, etc. In impersonal control planning and execution are separate, the conduct of the work may be regulated by automated control systems designed as part of the technology involved. The second aspect of this classification distinguishes between unitary control, in which a centrally integrated system exists which monitors and regulates standards and performances throughout the organization, and fragmented control in which standards, limits and goals may be set by several departments. In the latter case the completion of a particular task would involve the balancing of possibly conflicting demands e.g. between cost control and quality control. Here work is an important reminder that organizational problems can only be adequately studied in the real-life context in which they occur and that there are considerable dangers in attempting to generalize on the basis of solutions which were found to be effective in a particular organizational setting.

The impact of technology and technological change

upon the work group and its relations within the total organization has been examined at length in the work of Trist and his associates (e.g. Trist and Bamforth, 1951; Emery and Trist, 1960, 1965). In conceptualizing the organization as 'an open socio-technical system', this work has demonstrated the value of the systems' approach in organizational analysis, from the level of the effects of social and psychological pressures upon the individual worker to that of the examination of the enterprise as a whole. A general introduction to the systems approach is provided by Jenkins and Youle (1971) and a selection of systems contributions to organizational analysis is to be found in Emery's book *System Thinking* (1969).

In a more general sense it should be borne in mind that no enterprise, however compact and clearly structured its organization chart, is a truly independent social unit. If the enterprise is one of a group of companies it is probable that certain important aspects of policy are determined at group board level and that there are consequent constraints upon the freedom of decisions and control within the individual member companies. In this situation it is also possible that events outside the control of the individual company, such as failure or success in other member companies of the group, could influence its activities.

Even if the enterprise is a single unit, the activities of other formal structures will impinge upon it. Its freedom of decision may be restricted by its participation in agreements with local or national trade or employers' associations so that the organization itself, as a member of such a grouping, may be subject to norms and sanctions bearing upon its policies or practices.

It is also probable that a further series of operating constraints will exist as a result of agreements between the organization and the trades unions and professional associations which represent its employees, governing such aspects as pay, conditions of work, employment practices etc.

Even in the simplest of cases, it is probable that our organization chart, at the formal level of description, will tell only part of the story. The individuals shown by the chart to occupy positions within the organization will most probably be simultaneously members of other formal organizations as a direct result of their employment. Such memberships exercise important influences on their behaviour in their work situation. The organization itself, as has been mentioned, is in turn subject to influences arising both from its associations with other groups and from local, national and international economic and financial factors entirely outside its control.

Informal dynamics

What the organization chart does not show

Even when the chart gives an accurate and up-to-date representation of the formal structure of an organization, it does not give a full picture of its activities or the full pattern of communications or role relationships which exist within it.

Some examples, drawn from actual cases, may illustrate this point. In our simplified section of an organization chart (Fig. 4.2) we have a board of six directors plus a managing director, four departmental managers, a general foreman, three foremen and thirty shop-floor workers; the levels of authority and lines of communication are conventionally represented.

Situation 1. The managing director is nearing retirement, has been in failing health for some time, and has been assisted in his duties by director 1, a much younger man, who will eventually succeed him. For practical purposes, effective lines of communication have been developed between director 1 and departmental managers 1, 3 and 4; departmental manager 2, however, is elderly and has been a friend of the managing director for many years. He does not like director 1 and has described him as 'a young interloper'. Consequently, he communicates with him as little as possible and prefers to pass information to the managing director whenever he can.

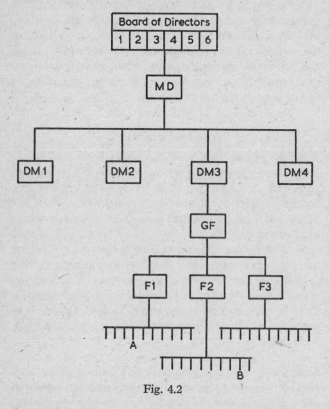

Fig. 4.2

Situation 2. Departmental manager 1 is regarded as of limited capability. Development is to take place in his area of the organization but he has expressed reluctance to increase his work load and the directors doubt whether he would be able to do so. He may soon leave the organization.

Situation 3. Departmental manager 3 is regarded by his superiors as 'a high flyer'. Director 1 in particular sees him as a potential future member of the board.

Situation 4. Departmental manager 4 is the nephew of director 6 and the newest member of the management team. In fact, his uncle does not particularly like him and has studiously avoided showing any kind of favouritism. His managerial colleagues, however, feel that he has 'a private line to the board' and view him with some caution and suspicion.

Situation 5. Worker A is a competent operative; he is also an intelligent, enthusiastic and ambitious convener of shop stewards. His eventual ambition is to make a career as a trades union official.

Situation 6. Worker B does not own a car; he lives two doors away from foreman 3 and they have been friends for many years. Foreman 3 drives him to work every day. In the course of conversation one morning, B talks about a tooling problem which had held up his work on the previous day and later foreman 3 mentions the problem in the hearing of the general foreman. The general foreman does not like foreman 2, B's immediate superior, and takes him to task for not reporting the problem. Foreman 2 is now under the impression that B or foreman 3 'are out to make trouble'.

Each of the six situations described above is real; for convenience they have been brought together in the one organizational setting. None of them is in any way remarkable as a human situation; each of them, and many others of similar nature, could be found in any form of organizational setting. Any reader can relate this type of illustration to the organizational setting with which he is familiar: in doing so he is likely to find that his understanding of the situation is to a considerable degree dependent upon such networks of relationships. Their importance lies in the fact that they represent the informal dynamics which operate within any formal structure and which can influence in many ways the roles and relationships which exist in the organization; facilitating or inhibiting communication through the channels represented on the formal chart and creating informal channels which can considerably alter the form of the communication network within the organization. In a sense, any formal organization chart is an idealized model of the enterprise – how it should operate – but it would be a mistake to assume that it accurately represents the actual situation.

Personal and interpersonal factors

Organizations are composed of individuals and it is their normal behavioural variations, interacting with the formal structure of the situation, which determine the pattern of informal dynamics. No matter how clearly an organizational function is specified, it is unlikely that any two individuals in that situation will interpret their role in exactly the same way. Something of the individual personality is imposed upon the role, and both positive and negative relationships will develop between individuals within the organization; they may be influenced by job-related factors or may arise from off-the-job contacts.

The role of individual factors and the psychological level of analysis in the study of organizations is ignored by some organizational sociologists and misused by others. Although Thompson (1967) admits the possibility of some variation in human abilities and needs, such factors are seen as peripheral, and he is content to assume that organizational behaviour is governed by means of rationality. Blau places considerable reliance (in his studies of organizations as wholes) upon organization charts and those data that can be obtained from the records of organizations and interviews with key informants, without intensive observation or interviewing (Blau, 1956:333). He apparently finds no difficulty in generalizing from the latter source to attribute their ideas to all managers.

It might be considered that the practice of averaging out the views and attitudes of individual informants to produce 'typical' presentations of 'working class', 'middle class', 'blue collar', 'white collar' can in some instances be little better than a sophisticated form of stereotyping. The danger inherent in the uncritical use of reported attitudes is well illustrated in Sykes' (1964) study of attitudes and stereotypes among industrial workers in a heavy engineering plant. He found that the attitudes of workers towards foremen in general was extremely negative. When the interviews were extended to examine attitudes towards individual foremen with whom the workers had direct contact, a completely different picture emerged and reports were generally favourable. Sykes concluded that the initial response was to a negative stereotype of foremen, the origin of which lay in a period in the previous history of the plant when supervision had been strict to the point of brutality and sometimes corrupt. The foremen concerned had long since gone but the oral tradition had lived on and provided the basis for a stereotype which actually influenced the attitudes of workers who had never experienced the situation themselves.

A similar phenomenon was found in a study carried out by the author in 1968. A new factory on Tyneside had recruited former shipyard workers as the major part of its work force. Aware of the history of poor labour-management relations in some sections of local industry, the new management had spent much time and money in providing good working conditions and well-designed consultative machinery. They were surprised that the response of their new labour force seemed less than positive; a series of complaints were put forward which, although often trivial in themselves, were symptomatic of underlying tension and dissatisfaction. On investigation it appeared that the behaviour of the workers was fundamentally related to the attitudes towards management which they had brought with them into the new work situation. These attitudes were based not only upon past personal experience but also upon the oral tradition of the area that management is essentially exploitative and punitive. Instances in support of this attitude were offered which stretched back in time to the period of the Jarrow hunger marches when many of the men concerned had not even been born. The view was frequently expressed that if a management seems to offer something for nothing there must be a catch. Hence the testing-out behaviour of the successive minor complaints.

Research such as the study of personality determinants on the effects of participation by Vroom (1959) pointed to the need to consider the interaction of the personality characteristics of subordinates and different leadership patterns. Much work had also been carried out in exploring the complex relationships between the personality characteristics involved in leadership, in the interaction between the leader and the group and the relationships of situational variables to such factors (Stodgill, 1950; Mann, 1959; Fiedler, 1966). The importance of individual patterns of motivation in the understanding of behaviour in work settings has been extensively discussed in the work of Maslow (1954), Herzberg (1966), Vroom (1964, 1965) and Lock and Bryan (1968, 1969) (see E5). The effects of motivational factors has been shown to be significant at all levels within the organization.

Attempts at assessment and measurement of individual characteristics associated with performance in work situations have been extensive (see E2). Even if such approaches show that techniques in this area are less than perfect, there can be little doubt that the relevance of such personal variables to the behaviour produced in organizational settings has been clearly demonstrated (Cronbach and Glaser, 1965; Bray and Grant, 1966).

The evidence that attitudes, interests, personality factors, motivational variables and other individual differences can be important influences in behaviour in work settings is overwhelming. To attempt to understand organizational structure without taking such aspects into account in the analysis seems rather like trying to complete a complicated jigsaw puzzle without using all the pieces.

Informal group processes

The organization chart gives a clear indication of many formal groups within the enterprise. In our simplified chart, groups determined by the nature of their formal tasks or by their common levels of seniority within the structure would include the board of directors, the departmental managers, the foremen, and the workers. Subdivisions could be recognized, for example the three separate groups of workers under foremen 1, 2 and 3.

It would not necessarily follow that such formal associations of individuals would constitute groups in the psychological sense of the term. In a large organization it is possible that some managers, foremen or workers could carry out their normal activities without coming into contact with each other and without any real sense of social cohesion.

In this context the definition of a psychological group employed by Schein (1965) is of particular value, emphasizing the interaction of group members, their psychological awareness of each other and their perception of themselves as constituting a group. Formal groupings within an organization may reflect the patterns of association necessary for the performance of duties and tasks but they do not necessarily correspond to the patterns of association which arise as a function of human interactions; nor do they necessarily meet the needs of individuals for friendship, support, reality testing and a sense of social identity. Such informal group structures will arise whenever people are in relatively close and continuous contact, and their formation will not be entirely constrained by the relationships shown on the organization chart.

A further version of our simplified part of an organization chart (Fig. 4.3) and a few examples may help to illustrate this point.

Situation 1. Directors 4, 5 and 6, the managing director and departmental manager 2 constitute the 'old guard' of the management team. They have been members of the company for many years and set a high value upon the traditions, reputation and practices which have long been characteristic of management thinking in the organization. They constitute a clique with common attitudes and interests focused upon a wish to maintain the form of the company as they know it and to resist change.

Situation 2. Directors 1 and 2 and departmental managers 3 and 4 are relatively young and enthusiastic; they have active interests in organizational development and believe that the company has rested too long on the laurels of past achievements. They constitute a clique in conflict with that described in Situation 1.

Situation 3. The general foreman, foreman 3 and four workers constitute a further form of clique. They served their apprenticeships in the company many years ago and have remained with the firm ever since. Although they are, formally, in superior-subordinate relationships, the informal bond of their longstanding friendship has continued.

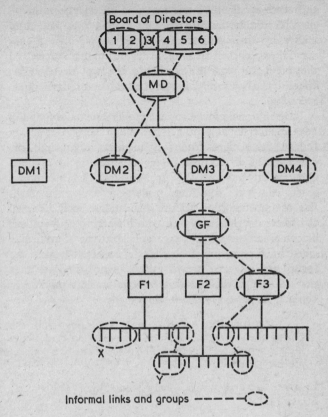

Informal links and groups ------○

Fig. 4.3

As we saw in Situation 6 (p. 59) the informal communication channels provided by such cliques can sometimes pass information more rapidly than the formal channels.

Situation 4. Group X and group Y are both part of the formal group of workers. Group X includes two members of the works' committee and all are active trades unionists;

they vote at all union meetings and attend classes in industrial relations in their free time. Group Y are bound together by their enthusiasm for racing pigeons; a substantial part of their free time is devoted to this activity and they are highly regarded members of the local pigeon-racing fraternity. They rarely, if ever, have time to attend union meetings.

Such informal groups and many more are to be found in any organizational setting; they are a normal result of human interactions. Attempts to prevent or limit the development of informal groups are likely to be resented and are rarely successful. Even in custodial institutions where efforts are sometimes made to formalize the activities of inmates by restrictive regulations, such informal structures develop with their own hierarchies and systems of communication. It is, perhaps, in this type of artificially constrained situation that the differences between the formal and informal structure of an organization are most marked due to the fact that the two systems may be in conflict. As Jones (1962 : 90–91) remarks:

> ... in correctional systems, one is dealing with the norms of the prison system on the one hand, and of the inmate system on the other. The goals of the two systems are incompatible.

In more general terms, Sherif and Sherif (1969 : 154) observe:

> To the extent that an organization functions adequately, it obviates the rise of informal groups within it whose leadership and status hierarchy are at variance with those of the formal organization.
>
> Conversely, to the extent that informal organization exists at variance with the formal structure and contrary to the formally instituted values, norms, or purposes, the inadequacy of the formal organization is indicated.

The possibilities of conflict between the formal and informal systems will be considered at a later stage but, even in normal conditions, the importance of recognizing the existence of the two systems must be stressed. The informal structure of an organization is a unique and dynamic phenomenon which can only be studied in the context of the working organization. If our view of an organization is based solely upon the static formal structure, our appreciation of the communication and activities which take place within it will be both partial and inaccurate.

5
Organizations in the public sector

In an earlier chapter we considered, in general terms, various types of organizational structure. To a degree this form of classification will indicate the nature of the internal dynamics most likely to be found within a particular organization, but, even in situations which seem to fit closely within one of the classical definitions, we may expect to find variations in the details of their day-to-day operation and their internal atmosphere or organizational climate. Although the general type of organization imposes certain formal constraints, the group interaction and role relationships of its members will also influence its functioning. Just as we can simultaneously recognize important similarities in people's behaviour and the essential uniqueness of the individual, so one can recognize and take practical account of similarities between organizations while remembering that the detailed functioning of each organizational unit is unique.

Public sector organizations, such as the Civil Service, local government, prisons, schools, hospitals etc, often appear to attract the interest of organizational sociologists as illustrations of institutions whose structure is basically bureaucratic; not infrequently the implicit suggestion is that the perceived social deficiencies of such institutions stem from the fact that bureaucratic necessarily means anti-people. Of course, such criticism can be justified; particularly when the goals of the organization cease to be the welfare of the community or special group which it is intended to serve, and become concerned with the maintenance of the system or the satisfaction of those needs of its members which conflict with its social role.

Perhaps the most important difference between industrial organizations and those in the public sector lies in the fact that the former are basically concerned in dealing with objects, the latter in dealing with people. In considering the internal social aspects of an industrial organization we are examining relationships within a hierarchy extending from the most junior worker to the most senior manager. In the public sector a further level of interaction exists, the people upon whom the function of the organization is exercised, whether they are pupils, prisoners, patients or the public in general. An industrial manager might feel that he was doing a good job if he had a successful balance of interests between producing a well-standardized, saleable product and maintaining a good level of job-satisfaction in his work force. It is rather more difficult to apply productivity targets or quality control to people, particularly when it is recognized that their human needs must be met as well as those of the members of the organization.

There is a further type of problem particularly relevant to the public sector organizations. As they exist in order to provide a service to people, should the public at large have a voice in defining their goals? The question is largely rhetorical as, whether or not the public has an effective voice in such matters, they certainly hold and express views on the goals of such organizations and on how best they should be attained. The problem lies in the discrepancies between the goals as perceived by the public, the members of the organizations and the planners and researchers. This problem will not be explored in detail here, but one or two examples may serve to illustrate the areas of difficulty.

Is the function of a prison to punish the criminal and confine him to ensure the safety of law-abiding citizens or is it to rehabilitate the offender so that he may become a useful member of society? Is the function of a psychiatric hospital to provide a safe confinement for 'abnormal' individuals so that society may be protected from them or is it to treat illness and enable the patient to take his place again in the community? It is probable that each of these views would have its advocates in the range of public opinion but, if they are regarded as ranges of opinion, the general public would tend to favour the 'protection of society' view whereas practitioners and researchers in the fields concerned would be more likely to favour the 'treatment' view.

Public opinion on such issues does not invariably provide a reliable guide; as has been mentioned, expressed attitudes are not necessarily reliable predictors of actual behaviour, nor are the attitudes necessarily consonant with each other (see B3). In an unpublished preliminary inquiry on the feasibility of setting up a 'half-way house' in a residential area to give discharged long-stay psychiatric patients the opportunity of re-adjusting to society in a partially sheltered environment on first leaving hospital, the following observations were made: 64 per cent of a sample of 200 local residents thought that the idea was good in principle but only 20 per cent felt that their neighbourhood was a suitable location. It was later noted that 15 per cent of those who had expressed support for the idea were signatories of a public petition against it when a formal proposal was made.

Generalizations about either people or institutions are likely to be misleading. Even when the stated goals are the same, there are wide variations in the actual practices of both our illustrative categories. Some hospitals have modern techniques but nineteenth-century attitudes in their relations with people; some are less well-equipped but function as genuinely therapeutic communities. Some prisons and sections within them may do more harm than good to their inmates, others discharge a real, if sometimes limited, rehabilitative function.

A final general point applies to both our examples of institutions: under some styles of management their structural characteristics allow a quite considerable degree of autonomy in day-to-day control to members of staff in charge of sub-units within the organization. The attitudes which a particular prison officer or ward sister brings to the interpretation of his or her role can have a considerable effect on the psychological climate of the section of the organization for which they are responsible. The effect of this combination of functional autonomy and individual role interpretation is generally more marked in the institution than in an industrial setting where structural constraints are generally less, social interaction is less limited, and rule systems are less rigid.

Schools

Any consideration of the study of schools as organizations soon reveals that, although the history of this field of research is relatively short, it is complex and to some extent confused. Hoyle (1969, 1973) reviews a wide range of organizational research in schools and school administration; our present outline concentrates upon some of the major areas of interest and difficulty.

One line of development can be traced through studies of educational administration in the United States, reflecting in its early stages the influence of the scientific management approach and following the change of emphasis to the human relations views of the 1930s and 1940s. The 1950s produced the so-called 'new movement' characterized by increased sophistication in theory-building to research, but, in Hoyle's words.

> although the new movement aimed to be interdisciplinary, the major figures in the field tended to be educational psychologists whose focus was leadership, morale and communication rather than formal structure, goals and culture. (1969)

The contribution of the organizational sociologists remained to a considerable degree separate from this new development; partly due to differences in approach, not only between sociology and other disciplines, but within sociology itself. Some researchers saw schools as additional forms of organizations providing opportunities for extending and testing general theory in organizational sociology. Others, concerned with the need to offer relevant predictions and applications, sought to construct theory from the data of the situations studied (Glaser and Strauss, 1968). The distinction between research directed towards the construction of general theory and that which seeks to find solutions to actual problems is important; the teacher may tend to see the former contribution as less relevant to his needs than the latter.

Although American research in both educational administration and the school itself has exercised considerable influence on British studies, there are significant differences in educational structure, custom and practice in the two countries. Studies such as the examination of the exercise of power in schools by Lutz and Iannaccone (1969), and Owens' (1970) examination of organizational behaviour, clearly show both the lack of structural comparability and the relevance of behavioural findings.

In Britain the situation is further complicated by the fact that several major areas of research in educational organizations are political battle-grounds. Comprehensive schools, de-streaming, the fate of public and grant-aided schools, are all sensitive political issues. It is only too apparent that many of the arguments advanced for and against such issues owe more to political and emotional commitment than to the detachment of the researcher. In view of the substantial demands which education makes upon national resources, it would be unreasonable to expect that education should be kept out of politics. The influence of the views of protagonists of the right and the left, however, may make one regret that politics cannot be kept out of education.

The view that the schools should be used to destroy our existing corrupt society and then to build a new one (Duane, 1968) has not been without influence upon some educational commentators and researchers. The same could be said for the opposed view:

> We must reject the chimera of equality and proclaim the ideal of quality. The egalitarian, whose ideas of 'social justice' are prescriptions for mediocrity and anarchy, must be prevented from having any control over the education of the young. (Maude, 1971)

Emotional involvement with a cause can obscure the real problems. A more balanced view is taken by Cleugh, who comments:

> There is a basic dishonesty of thought in the unwillingness abroad at present to face the facts that different children have different educational needs – or rather, to face it halfway as far as high-fliers are concerned, and to refuse to consider the obverse of the picture. Much of the so-called non-streaming is simply a denial that difficulties exist: by lumping all children together the problems are swept under the carpet. But to make problems less noticeable is not the same as solving them. (1971: 135)

A suitable final comment on this topic is provided by Burt:

... like every other human institution, English education has many imperfections. But the remedies are to be ascertained, not by armchair deductions from the theories of politicians or social reformers, but by constant trial and error, guided, supervised, and tested by scientific research. (1969:25)

Research approaches
It is difficult to categorize the different classes of contribution – or potential contribution – to the understanding of the social dynamics of schools as organizations. British studies in the traditions of organizational psychology or organizational sociology are few; the need to examine the interrelationship of formal and informal structures and processes within the school and its relationships with its environment has yet to be met. It is possible, however, to identify general areas in which valuable, if partial, contributions have been made, and to cite a few examples of the types of investigation which have been undertaken.

1. *Studies of internal issues related to the social aspects of the school organization.*
a) The attitudes of children, their relationships and cultural norms, and their friendship patterns have been investigated by Barker Lunn (1970), Hargreaves (1967) and Ford (1969). Although the findings are not uniform, there is a degree of agreement on such general observations as the tendency of children to choose their friends from those in the same social and ability groups as themselves, and the tendency for the children of parents in higher social class occupations to constitute a higher proportion of the upper stream groups.

Such studies are often treated as pieces of social research in their own right, rather than as contributions to the study of organizational issues. Research into factors such as the interaction between the informal structures of class groups, the formal structure of the school, and the influence of successive teachers upon the group could be of considerable interest.

b) The influences of administrative procedures and educational practices upon the children have been studied. Several researchers have investigated the effects of streaming, e.g. Lacey (1966). The observations of Barker Lunn (1970) to the effect that streaming does not influence academic attainment, should be read in conjunction with the comments of Lynn (1971), both because of the methodological issues involved and as an example of the controversial treatment of this topic.

The investigation of Hargreaves (1967), mentioned above, and that of Lacey (1970) on related samples, explore the relationships between streaming and factors such as achievement, opportunity and social stratification.

c) The nature of interactions between the teacher and the class, although studied by Wragg (1970) primarily in relation to the training of teachers, could be an area of considerable interest and the method of interaction analysis employed (Flanders, 1965) is a valuable tool in the examination of the organizational climate of classes and schools. The relationships between teacher style and effectiveness have been reviewed by Pidgeon (1970) and Flanders (1970). The effects of personal characteristics, role interpretation, teaching style and techniques deserve more attention. Traditional, attainment-oriented teaching can be challenging in one case, oppressive in another; learning by discovery can stimulate insight and enthusiasm in one situation, near-anarchy and mystification in another. The models of investigations of management styles could be of value here.

d) The attitudes and opinions of teachers constitute a further area of considerable relevance to the organizational dynamics of the school. Teachers' and parents' conceptions of the teacher's role were investigated by Musgrove and Taylor (1965) in terms of rated tasks and objectives. Teachers tended to lay stress upon the moral and intellectual aspects of the role and to show indifference to the social aims of education. The role conceptions of teachers in secondary modern schools and junior schools in working-class areas were more diffuse than those of grammar school teachers and teachers in junior schools in middle class areas. Not surprisingly there were discrepancies between teachers' and parents' conceptions of the role. Cane and Schroeder (1970) investigated the areas and topics of research regarded by teachers as immediate priorities and found general agreement that the topic of greatest importance was that of teachers and training.

It is a curious phenomenon that the groups within public sector institutions which have received least attention from researchers are the rank and file members – possibly the most important level at which to gain an understanding of the social dynamics of the organization. Not enough is known about the attitudes, job-satisfactions, role relationships, etc., of such groups as prison officers, police officers, nurses, teachers, etc.

A few studies relate such factors to organizational dimensions. The characteristics of head teachers and the resultant differences in organizational climate have been touched upon by Halpin (1966) and a typology of teachers is suggested by Rose and Martin (1974) with comment on role interpretation and teaching styles. Revans (1965) points to relationships between children's attitudes to teachers and teachers' attitudes to authority structures, suggesting that teachers who feel that they have a hand in the running of the school or that their problems are understood tend to be liked by pupils and seen as effective teachers; those who perceive authority as remote or dictatorial tend to be seen by pupils as unfriendly and ineffective.

In general, however, Hoyle's comment (1973:49), to the effect that British research in this area tends to focus upon the pupil dimension, is still true.

2. *Case studies of schools*

It is, perhaps, in this area that one might expect to find material which would make comparisons between schools and other types of organizations which have been studied in depth; but the methods of organizational analysis used elsewhere do not appear to have made any great impact on the British educational system. More typical of the work in this area is the study by King (1969), mainly concerned with class, the transmission of cultural values and pupil involvement in a grammar school. The approach of Wakeford (1969) in his study of public schools does not set out to test hypotheses but rather to describe the essential qualities of this type of school on a basis of participant observation extended by comparative illustrations from sociological theory. Only a few studies have attempted to apply organizational concepts to the formal properties of schools, e.g. Turner (1969).

3. *Comparative studies of schools*

The majority of the studies available in this area are of the survey type, so that although they provide interesting statistical data, they do not constitute organizational analyses of the schools concerned. Kalton's (1966) study of a large number of public schools falls into this category. Interest has been concentrated more upon comparison of methods and results, in the tradition of educational rather than organizational research.

The investigation by Lambert (1975) of public schools has to some extent changed its nature during its development – possibly due in part to the fact that the senior author became a headmaster during the course of the study. It offers a detailed consideration of the aims of residential education, and some evaluation of the differences in instrumental and organizational styles in different types of school. The data employed was obtained from questionnaires, scales – as described in Lambert *et al* (1970) –

interviews, factual and documentary material, diaries and the evidence of the Public Schools Commission. Such studies frequently point to apparently significant similarities and differences between organizations, but in summarizing observations from several sources the internal dynamics of individual situations can be obscured rather than illuminated.

4. *The school in relation to its environment*

The consideration of the social context in which the school exists is, perhaps, of even more importance in the understanding of its operation than in the corresponding case of an industrial organization. There are numerous external constraints on its activities, in terms of both legislation and goals in the form of examinations, which are determined by outside bodies. The social characteristics of the neighbourhood served by the schools will be a significant influence as will the attitudes and expectations of the parents. In the latter context, observations such as that of Barker Lunn (1970) that 65 per cent of parents of children in non-streamed schools and 79 per cent of those with children in streamed schools are in favour of streaming, deserve more systematic attention than they have received. Peaker (1967) showed that parental attitudes rather than home circumstances were the important determinants of school progress and that the influence of differences between schools and between teachers was less than that of either of the previous factors. Further examination of home environment by Fraser (1969) identified normal home background, emotional stability, freedom from tension and economic insecurity, and consistent encouragement by parents as necessary conditions if the child is to reach the level of attainment allowed by his intelligence.

Such work gives a clear indication of the importance of environmental factors but is again closer to the traditional methods of British educational research than to the more dynamic treatments of the relations between the organization and environment developed in American studies.

5. *Educational administration*

In reviewing organizational theory and educational administration, Hoyle (1969) considered that, as the multi-disciplinary approach to educational administration has not yet yielded balanced contributions from the separate behavioural sciences, we should, in this country, 'Advance along mono-disciplinary paths in the hope that a multi-disciplinary approach will eventually emerge.' It might be considered that mono-disciplinary paths are rather more likely to lead to mono-disciplinary types of conclusion.

The tendency has been to examine isolated aspects of the administrative process or to study particular roles. In his review of role theory and educational administration, Burnham acknowledges the importance of role theory as a tool of analysis in organizational settings but mentions in a footnote:

> Throughout the chapter, illustrations will be largely concerned with the role of the headmaster. There is no intention, however, to limit the relevance of role theory to this one position; the head is used as one example from a whole range of administration in the field of education. (1969:73)

This tendency to concentrate upon single roles has limited the range of organizational analysis possible and has been followed by other researchers in the field, e.g. Cohen (1970).

Research in this area seems to suffer from lack of co-ordination and a multiplicity of conceptual bases rather than from any lack of enthusiasm or interest. It is difficult to compare studies in which the frames of reference range from the educational measurement approach of the 1920s to the most recent – and sometimes imperfectly tested – developments in educational and organizational theory.

An initial complication in examining the organizational characteristics of a hospital arises from its basic structural peculiarities. In the place of the more usual single hierarchical structure of an industrial organization we find three main distinct but interrelated hierarchies – administrative, medical and nursing – in addition to a number of related sub-systems represented by ancillary services with varying degrees of functional autonomy. The psychiatric hospital may have a duplicate nursing hierarchy of separate male and female staffs. It has been suggested that this inevitably produces the problems characteristic of large organizations composed of several sub-systems – delay in decision processes, problems of ego-satisfaction for the majority of the individuals involved and problems for the subordinate members arising from the exercise of bureaucratic power (Anderson and Warkow, 1961). Revans (1962) has commented upon further concerns which are becoming increasingly evident in the current problems of the health services; difficulties in communication between different professional groups and between status groups within each profession. Such factors are illustrated in the increasing activity of ancillary staff unions, not only in relation to pay and conditions of work, but also in relation to the general policy of the health services, e.g. with regard to the continued existence of private beds in National Health Service hospitals. The adoption of industrial action by nursing staffs in support of pay claims, and the tendency for professional associations of medical staffs to develop the characteristics of trade unions, also indicate significant changes in this area.

In such situations change takes place in the norms of the group concerned reflecting the conflict between individual aspirations, group loyalties, the constraints of traditional organizational structure and the changes occurring in the socio-economic environment. To suggest that a nursing career is based upon a special sense of vocation and is, therefore, fundamentally different from other types of work, is no longer seen as justification for wages and conditions of work which compare unfavourably with those found in other work with a comparable level of training and responsibility. The changing attitudes of the group are seen in a reduced tendency for restrictive rules to be accepted simply because they have always been a traditional part of nursing training, particularly when the rule in question seems to have lost whatever relevance it once possessed. On the basis of Weber's description of a bureaucracy, it may be suggested that the number of formal rules which exist in an organization, and in particular the number which continue to be applied after they have outlived their usefulness, can serve as an indicator of the rigidity of the structure of that organization.

It has been noted in other organizational contexts that the disadvantages of being a member of a large organization tend to decrease as one is promoted within its structure (Forehand and Gilmer, 1964) and that opportunities for satisfaction tend to increase with seniority (Porter and Lawler, 1965). It seems to be true in the hospital context that dissatisfaction has first become evident in the lower levels of the hierarchies in the increased tendency to seek the support of trades union membership and in the emergence of separate bodies representing the interests of the junior levels within professional groups, e.g. the Junior Hospital Doctors' Association.

More recently, the work-to-rule of some hospital consultants in opposition to the intended modification of their conditions of service is a further indication of dissatisfaction, illustrating the point made in the introductory chapter that external changes – in this case government policy – can influence organizational behaviour.

When an organization with a highly traditional and

hierarchical structure becomes subject to pressure from social change in its external environment, the problems for management are considerable. The application of modern management techniques to the formal aspects of the structure can provide only a partial answer. More important to identify and more difficult to approach are the informal processes existing within the system: problems associated with communication, status differential, prejudice and job satisfaction must be examined and understood if technical developments in management are to be implemented effectively.

Even between hospitals of the same type it is difficult to make comparisons in terms of goal definition and goal achievement. The effect upon the structure and function of the hospital of different 'psychiatric ideologies' can mean that goals, treatment priorities and professional relationships are evaluated in very different ways (Strauss et al, 1964).

Although it is not the purpose of this chapter to discuss personal and interpersonal factors in detail, it should be remembered that the differing management styles of the leaders of the hospital hierarchies can play an important part in influencing the dynamics of the organization as a whole. There is reason to believe not only that different organizational goals seem to require different patterns of interpersonal relationship and different leadership styles (Roby, Nicol and Farrell, 1963), but also that there are individual differences in preferences for different styles of leadership (Forehand and Gilmer, 1964). Conflict between individual and organizational goals can be a factor of importance in its effect upon the direction or limitation of action within the organization (Simon, 1964). As already mentioned, however, interactions between the individual and the organization are determined to a significant degree by the characteristics of the organization itself, and models have been described in which the unit of study is the total organization with studies of individual and group processes contributing to an understanding of the total situation rather than constituting an end in themselves (Kahn *et al*, 1964).

Some hospitals certainly show many of the characteristics of bureaucratic structure described by Hall (1963), but there have been determined attempts to minimize the effects upon individuals within such formal structures both in the development of socially orientated therapeutic environments (Maxwell Jones, 1962) and in the attention drawn to the danger of a too successful adaptation by patients to the restricted environment of the psychiatric hospital (Barton, 1959). It is not beyond the bounds of possibility that the phenomenon of 'institutional neurosis' described by Barton may have a parallel in the effects of some hospital environments upon staff as well as upon chronic patients. To adapt too thoroughly to the supporting and constraining systems of one organization may limit one's potential to respond to changes in the environment.

The identification and definition of the organizational goals of a hospital present certain difficulties. The system of classification of organizations in terms of who benefits from their activities, suggested by Blau and Scott (1963), offers one possible basis. Writing on hospitals for the mentally retarded, Pauline Morris (1969) suggested that, although it might be natural to assume that hospitals are service organizations existing for the benefit of their clientele, subnormality hospitals could more readily be regarded as commonweal organizations exercising a custodial function for the benefit of society. Arguably, the latter classification could be applied to some aspects of the function of psychiatric hospitals and those which care for the chronically ill.

A real need exists to examine and evaluate the organizational goals of hospitals and the several ways in which the same goal can be interpreted by the personnel involved.

Only when goals have been clearly identified can the contribution of particular activities and working practices be evaluated in terms of their contribution to the work of the hospital as a whole. The increasing complexity of the structure of health and social service organizations has led to lack of clarity in the interpretation of goals and to failure of communication within and between systems with consequent areas of duplication of effort and gaps where no effective service is provided. Titmus (1958) foresaw one of the special problems of this area when he speculated that hospitals 'may tend increasingly to be run in the interests of those working in and for the hospital rather than in the interests of the patients'. Cartwright (1964) saw some aspects of general hospitals as 'legacies from the era of charity and custodial care', pointing to factors such as failure to recognize the patients' need for explanation, clinical teaching which takes no account of the patient's feelings in the situation, and attitudes of condescension and lack of consideration by consultants who keep patients waiting.

Problems remain to be resolved in this area, highlighted by pressures from both staff and patient groups. Change is necessary in many areas of the health and social services and much progress has already been made. In highly traditional and hierarchical organizations of this type, however, the process is neither rapid nor painless.

6
Climate and conflict in organizations

The concept of organizational climate

In the introductory comments on organizations the point was made that it is essentially unrealistic to think of any enterprise as if it existed in a vacuum. An important aspect of the social dynamics of an organization is the environment in which it operates and with which it interacts. In many respects, an organization must be able to respond appropriately to the environment in which it exists in order to survive.

Just as the total organization must be understood in its external context, so an adequate appreciation of the social processes which occur within the organization requires us to consider the nature of the internal environment. This internal environment, or 'climate' as it has come to be called, presents quite considerable problems of definition; possibly because, although it is not difficult to accept the idea that an organization possesses a characteristic atmosphere or 'feel', it seems to be perceived in differing ways by different individuals. Some seem to be more or less sensitive to aspects of climate than others: a characteristic which appears positive to one member of an organization may be perceived as negative or unsatisfactory by someone else.

Consider the choice between working in one or other of the following settings:

1. 'This job presents an ideal opportunity for the energetic, enthusiastic and determined young man. As a member of our sales team your opportunities are unlimited. The field is highly competitive and only the toughest can make the grade, but for the successful, aggressive sales executive the rewards are great.'

2. 'In this post your initial salary is dependent upon age and qualifications. During the early years of your career you will have training opportunities which will enable you to qualify for promotion to higher grades with commensurately higher salary scales. The conditions of work are stable and secure and there is generous pension provision on retirement.'

Admittedly ignoring many aspects of the two hypothetical situations, it seems reasonable to assume that the working atmosphere of the two jobs would be rather different. In so far as this is suggested in the two brief descriptions which give some suggestion of the kinds of demands facing the potential employee and the kinds of relationships he would be likely to encounter, you may feel that one or other of the jobs is potentially attractive to you. It is likely that if your initial impression is that the characteristics of job 1 appear to you as exciting and challenging, job 2 may seem limiting and uninspiring: if job 2 seems attractive due to security and a clearly defined ladder of promotion, job 1 could well seem stressful and uncertain.

For the present purpose it is sufficient to say that the two situations are likely to provide two rather different kinds of organizational climate.

Gilmer (1971) considers different aspects of climate and

offers the definition that it is 'those characteristics that distinguish the organization from other organizations and that influence the behavior of people in the organization'.

The definition favoured by Georgopoulos (1965) suggests that the organization is best regarded as a specialized group situation and that climate is determined by the normative behavioural standards and attitudes which direct activity within the organization and on the bases of which the individual may interpret the situation.

Meyer (1967) lays emphasis upon management style and the policies and operating conditions of the organization.

Other definitions stress different aspects of the situation, overlapping in varying degrees with each other. In general, formal structural factors such as the type of organization, the technology concerned, company policies, formal operational goals and operating rules seem to form one group of factors. Another group includes informal social factors such as attitudes, value systems, forms of social behaviour which are encouraged or sanctioned, and ways in which conflict is handled. Particular aspects of the organization as it impinges upon the individual have been emphasized including support, tolerance, warmth, freedom of action and job-satisfaction. Individual factors have also been seen as relevant; including the personality, management style and goals of influential members of the organization, the ways in which individual members perceive their work environment and the constraints and reward systems governing their work behaviour.

Many of the studies carried out in this field have adopted a factor analytic approach – a mathematical technique designed to describe variables in terms of basic factors, derived from the analysis of correlations between measures of the variables – but, due to the wide variety of ways in which the problem has been defined and the variation in methods of data collection, it is often difficult to make valid comparisons between the findings of different researchers. Some have obtained their information from managers, some from workers, some from all levels within the organization, others have used their own observations. The information gathered in different studies has included actual practices, preferred practices, ideal practices and practices perceived as important. Different aspects of the work situation have been examined, including control systems, communication systems, reward systems, work-group organization and role relationships. In short, the range and complexity of the variables hypothesized as being relevant to a definition of organizational climate have been considerable.

Campbell *et al* (1970) have offered a composite view of the factors which seem to recur in investigations, and identify four general headings:

1. *Individual autonomy*. This facet includes such elements as individual responsibility, independence, orientation towards rules and freedom of individual initiative; essentially the decision-making power of the individual.

2. *The degree of structure imposed upon the position*. This category covers a range of structural constraints upon direction, objectives and the nature of supervision. They identify the major element as 'the degree to which the objectives of, and methods for, the job are established and communicated to the individual by superiors'.

3. *Reward orientation*. This appears to be a rather loose grouping of a range of reward-related elements including not only the formal aspects of reward but also satisfaction and 'promotion-achievement orientation'.

4. *Consideration, warmth and support*. Campbell *et al* see this category as less clear than the preceding three, possibly

because of the variation in the definitions applied to similar terms by different investigators, possibly because the factors involved have been studied in different ways and at different levels of superior/subordinate and peer relationships within the organization. It might also be suggested that this category is particularly prone to be interpreted in different ways as a result of individual differences in the personalities of the individuals concerned.

It may be that part of the difficulty in defining the phenomenon or organizational climate is due to the complex involvement of components which are related to both the formal and informal aspects of structure, control systems, rules and norms and interpersonal relationships. Many of the contributory elements can be defined objectively but the climate impinges on the individual essentially as subjectively perceived, affective experiences. Attempts to describe it in purely objective terms are unlikely to give a complete picture and, as we do not have organizations composed of 'ideal' members who perceive the affective aspects of their environment with uniform accuracy, there is likely to be quite a wide variation in the ways in which the climate of the organization is perceived by individual members. In practice, then, judgements of organizational climate are usually based upon the most frequently occurring elements in the responses of the individual members of the organization being studied.

A further problem arises from the fact that not only may the same aspects of an organization be perceived differently by different individuals, but rules, sanctions and control systems can be interpreted in very different ways by those who operate them. This can lead to a series of microclimates within the same setting so that a description based on a process of averaging-out over the whole range of organizational functioning could obscure as much as it clarifies. This is readily observed in the different atmospheres of similar sections of the same organization – in industry, in hospital wards, in school classrooms etc. This involves more than differences in leadership styles as it can be manifest in attitudes, activities and relationships on a wider basis than the conventional leadership role. The personality characteristics of individuals who are influential in the social dynamics of the group, whether formally or informally, can influence the climate of the situation.

Conflict

General views of conflict

In general terms two different models of conflict are recognizable. These have been summarized by Kelly (1969: 500) as the human relations view and the realistic view; he outlines a number of aspects characteristic of each position which are summarized and paraphrased below.

The human relations view of conflict (Kelly)

1. Conflict, by definition, is avoidable. This follows from the presumption that organizations are stable, well-integrated units in which policy rests upon a basis of consensus. In this context, conflict would be an abnormal disturbance of the natural homeostatic equilibrium of the organization.

2. The causes of conflict are explicable in terms of personal idiosyncracies. If the natural equilibrium is disturbed, the cause is likely to be the inappropriate disruptive activity of some ill-disposed individual or group.

3. The organization rests upon a basis of legalistic authority. It would follow that problems should be resolved by the exercise of authority and that the role of the subordinate is to comply with the rules.

4. Social and organizational arrangements favour the legitimization of scapegoating and other methods of channelling off aggression. Kelly mentions university rag days as an example of this process. The reported Japanese practice of

providing a room where the employee can relieve his emotions by breaking crockery or punching a dummy figure would probably fall into this category.

5. The institutions for regulating conflict are inadequately developed.

6. When conflict arises, reactions to it tend to be inappropriate. Attempts are made to evade the issue, severally by denying its existence, by attempts at rationalization, in providing 'safe' explanations, and by suppression. When the issue can no longer be evaded, attempts are made to defer the discussion of the problem or to distract attention from it.

7. Polarization of perceptions, sentiments and behaviour. When finally confronted with an inescapable situation of overt conflict, perceptions of the issues and antagonists tend to extremes and are expressed in stereotyped terms. Emotional stress tends to reach a level at which it interferes with normal behaviour. The more committed members of opposed factions move apart to a position in which effective communication between them is difficult and overt aggression may emerge.

Kelly then proceeds to offer, in contrast, a further composite view of conflict:

A realistic view of conflict (Kelly)

1. Conflict is inevitable: it must be recognized and accepted as 'integral to any human encounter'. Conflict and change are seen as being inevitably interlocked as any redistribution of power and privilege will be sought by some and resisted by others.

2. The causes of conflict are to be found in the structural factors which determine the total situation. Four levels at which conflict arises are identified:

a) The individual level. Resting directly upon the frustration-aggression hypothesis of Dollard (1939) (see D2) to the effect that the occurrence of aggressive behaviour presupposes the existence of frustration and that the existence of frustration always leads to some form of aggression, Kelly argues that the universal aggressive potential of the individual linked to frustration will be a basic source of conflict.

b) The group level. The presumption is that there will be an asymmetrical distribution of satisfaction of needs among members who do not share the same value system (cf. *Relative Deprivation*, Merton, 1957), e.g. the concept that evaluation of one's wellbeing is not made in absolute terms but relative to the conditions, possessions, privileges, etc. of others.

c) The organizational level. Conflict may be expected between hierarchical levels and between functions e.g. as a result of differences in goal evaluation and need priorities.

d) The societal level. Conflict between classes and ethnic groups.

3. Conflict is recognized as a necessary element in change. Here Kelly extends the first point of his categorization in stating that change and its associated conflict are normal aspects of life in any advanced technological society.

4. A minimal level of conflict is optimal. Here Kelly argues for the desirability of a minimal level of conflict on the grounds that a change-free environment is unacceptable to the subjects in experimental situations. It might be considered that more appropriate support for this point would be found in the work on personality dynamics and effective behaviour in which the stimulating effect of a slight level of anxiety was noted and distinguished from the progressively more disruptive effects of increasing anxiety (Coleman, 1960).

5. Social science can be mobilized to find solutions to conflict problems.

6. The recognition that countries which failed to deal with conflict effectively have atrophied.

In presenting the above models, and in particular in his

'realistic view of conflict' Kelly appears to have been influenced by the view that conflict is basically structural in origin (Dahrendorf, 1958). He has extended this description by introducing other elements – the concept of relative deprivation, the frustration-aggression hypothesis and a bio-social view of the different classes of conflict situations. The main interests of this composite picture are the demonstrations of the generality of conflict as a social phenomenon and of the possibility of examining the process at various levels, from the individual to the societal.

Conflict at the individual level

Conflict as an aspect of individual experience could be regarded as a normal concomitant of existence. When we hesitate between two possible courses of action or in the choice of which of several possible goals is preferable, we are in a conflict situation. If we cannot resolve it, or avoid it, we must adapt to it to the best of our ability. It is probably true to say that we become aware of this type of situation not simply because conflict has arisen but due to difficulty experienced in the process of resolution or adaptation. For the individual, conflict itself is not uncomfortable or unpleasant but the frustration or anxiety associated with an unresolved conflict may be so.

The consideration of conflict as a part of individual behaviour should also serve as a reminder that, although we may set out to study behaviour in the work situation, the life experience of the individual does not fall neatly into such conventional divisions. Conflict, frustration, stress and anxiety can arise in any aspect of our lives; in so far as such events have an effect upon our behaviour, this can be carried over from the situation in which the problem arose to another. In simple terms, you do not leave your problems at the factory gates either when you come to work or when you go home; domestic difficulties can influence work behaviour and vice versa.

A further important aspect of this situation lies in the area of individual differences; both differences in abilities to resolve conflict situations and in the capacity to tolerate those which cannot be resolved. A conflict situation which is a stressful problem for one man could be seen as a stimulating challenge by another. Further, the capacity to tolerate stress, whether due to conflict or to other factors, varies from person to person and the threshold of tolerance for an individual may show variation through time and from one situation to another.

Conflict between individuals can also be of importance in organizational settings, particularly when those concerned occupy positions of authority within the structure of the enterprise. Such situations can arise not only as a result of disagreement in relation to work decisions but also from incompatibilities of personality. In so far as such conflict relates to power, the issue may be related directly to competition for recognized status within the organization but the issue can also be essentially personal, based possibly upon mutual antipathy. Although such interpersonal conflicts constitute part of the pattern of informal relationships in the work situation and may not be referable to any formal organization goal, their influence is very real and can interfere substantially with working relationships.

This aspect of interpersonal relationships is of particular relevance in team-building. It is easy to find examples of situations in which the addition of a new member to a team, particularly at management level, on the basis of his high qualifications and excellent experience has not only failed to improve group performance but possibly substantially reduced the efficiency of the group. Professional qualifications will be of little value if he is unacceptable in personal terms as a member of the group. In such a situation an acceptable new team member of adequate competence could be a preferable choice to a brilliant but socially incompatible candidate.

Role conflict
When there is a mis-match between an individual's role and his values, attitudes or beliefs, or between his role and the situation in which he finds himself, an imbalance is created. This inconsistency is a source of stress and the individual concerned is likely to seek some means of reducing it to a tolerable level. He may be able to modify the attitudes concerned so as to make them more compatible with his role, he may attempt to vary his interpretation of the role or he may abandon it altogether. This situation would be encountered, for example, by an authoritarian teacher transferred to a liberal school environment.

Such states of inconsistency are psychologically unpleasant and there is a tendency to attempt to reduce such effects when the type of conflict arises. Festinger's theory of cognitive dissonance (see B1, B3) suggests that we develop strategies to help us to reduce the unease associated with imbalances between attitudes and behaviour, generally by modifying the attitudes to increase their compatibility. The greater the inconsistency, the stronger the need to reduce the resultant psychological dissonance; this pressure is seen as being proportional to the importance of the elements concerned and to the proportion of the cognitive elements that are dissonant (Festinger, 1964). The terms employed are not clearly defined but the theory certainly points to a further area of conflict which is of importance in examining individual behaviour in group situations.

In evaluating this and other related 'equilibrium models', Sherif (1969:480) points to the inadequacy of simple 'hydraulic' and 'drive-reduction' analogues and states:

The psychological tendency towards stability proceeds over time on particular terms that can be defined as (1) the priority of values in the person's self-system, which is closely related to (2) the relative significance of his reference groups with their respective scales of values, and (3) the concrete interaction situation in which he goes about the business of living, earning a living, and maintaining a self-identity.

This comment strongly implies that the achievement of equilibrium is more complex than the currently available models would suggest.

Intra-group conflict

To the extent that any informal group develops its structure through the dynamic interactions of its members, it might be argued that conflict within the group is part of its normal developmental process and a feature that is likely to recur when group members compete for resources or prestige and when the group is affected by change. A group without internal conflict would be a group without internal change or one in which the response to change in the environment was invariably based upon the perfect consensus of its members: neither situation seems probable.

A distinction can be drawn between two general types of internal conflict: that in which the process seems closest to the form outlined above, in which adaptive development of the group takes place, and that which is maladaptive or potentially destructive to the life of the group.

In the first case, conflicts which relate to issues, values or goals which are essentially compatible with the existing standards of the group can have beneficial results. Such conflicts can lead to the clarification, extension or modification of group norms or to a reorganization of the internal relationships of the group without threatening its basic cohesion.

In the second case, conflict in which one or more of the issues involved is fundamentally at variance with the existing group standards can be disruptive. This process would be likely to lead to a weakening of the group structure through the development of competing factions and possible outcomes would include the splitting or total fragmentation of the group.

Like individuals, groups show differences in their ability to handle conflict situations or to tolerate their effects. Procedures may have been evolved for the purpose so that many conflict situations come to be handled in more or less agreed, conventional ways – the process has become institutionalized.

A further factor which contributes to such differences is the degree of cohesion of the group itself. This is a complex issue centring upon the observation that conflict occurring in a closely-integrated cohesive group is likely to be more intense in degree and more extensive in range. This seems to be due partly to the greater degree of affection and interpersonal involvement amongst group members. Initially this causes a suppression of conflict and of the expression of hostility, but if conflict becomes overt it seems to be intensified by the close involvement of group members and their knowledge of each other. Further, the suppressed material is re-activated, extending the area of conflict. This type of situation is illustrated by the intense nature of conflicts when they arise in family groups.

Inter-group conflicts

Group solidarity and group pride have often been regarded as positive elements of social behaviour, emphasizing the unity of effort directed towards group goals. It can also form a basis for conflict between groups. The 'us' and 'them' form of comparison, contrasting the high standards and goals of one's own group with those found elsewhere can be the basis of hostility and negative stereotyping characteristic of inter-group conflict. This process has long been recognized in the activities of propagandists who work to emphasize the perceived differences between groups by selective communications which emphasize (or invent) the positive attributes of the 'home' group and the negative characteristics of 'the enemy'. The techniques employed to produce such effects have reached a considerable degree of sophistication, not only in legalized conflict situations, such as war, but in a wide range of contrived or manipulated group rivalries in politics, religion, sport etc.

A considerable amount of experimental work has been carried out in this area, particularly by Sherif *et al.* Some of the conclusions from a series of experiments conducted in summer camps is summarized in Sherif and Sherif (1969:261); their findings include the following observations:

1. Inter-group conflict is not the result of neurotic or anti-social tendencies in group members; it can arise when the individuals concerned are 'normal, healthy and socially well-adjusted'.

2. Conflict between groups can enhance the level of co-operation within them but such democratic and co-operative characteristics are not directly transferable to relations between groups.

3. The nature of relations between groups can alter the internal structure and norms of the groups concerned. Conflict situations may bring about alterations in the status system of groups and produce new leaders.

4. Conflict between hostile groups does not appear to be reduced by contact as equals in pleasant, non-competitive situations.

5. When the groups engage in joint action towards some super-ordinate goal which cannot be achieved independently, co-operation can develop. A single instance of such co-operation, however, does not significantly alter the basic

level of inter-group conflict.

6. Successive activities of the type described in 5. above appear to lead to a reduction in the level of inter-group hostility and to patterns of joint co-operative activity.

7. Tools and techniques developed in group problem-solving and in conflict situations can also be used in co-operative activity.

8. Co-operative effort directed towards a super-ordinate goal alters the nature of both intra- and inter-group relationships and modifies norms and attitudes. Measures which failed to reduce conflict in conditions of open hostility come to be perceived in a more positive way.

Sherif answers the criticism that work carried out with groups of children may not be relevant to the adult situation, by citing the work of Blake and Mouton (1962) and Blake, Shepard and Mouton (1964). In a series of studies, these workers used the Sherif experiments as bases for the analysis of social interactions in adult groups; their findings indicate that the original experimental results and later extensions on similar bases have relevance for adult group situations.

The range of situations which could be classed as inter-group conflict is wide. The frustration of specific demands is a common characteristic of major conflict situations, where resolution centres upon achieving the specific goal in whole or in part. Other conflict situations lack clear goals and appear to be associated with the release of tension; although the conflict may seem to be an end in itself in this type of situation, the safety-valve function of such activities can be of value.

There are considerable differences between structures in the extent to which they are capable of institutionalizing or tolerating conflict. The more closed and rigid the organizational structure, the less likely it is that it can accommodate conflict without suffering damage. In extreme situations a sufficiently intense conflict can destroy the rigid structure within which it arises.

Organizational conflict

Any of the classes of conflict outlined above can exist in an organizational setting, and the comments on the inverse relationship between structural rigidity and the capacity to institutionalize or tolerate conflict are of particular relevance here. Both the formal and the informal aspects of the organization can be involved, and any effective analysis must recognize the existence and the importance of both aspects of the structure.

Conflict can arise between different hierarchical levels within the same structure; not only between management and shop-floor workers, but also between different management groups, e.g. marketing and production; between staff specialists and line managers; between the conflicting interests of specialist groups in 'empire-building' situations; between trades unions, e.g. demarcation disputes; and within the same union, e.g. between union officials and an unofficial strike committee.

It is also possible to find situations in which the antagonists in what was originally an inter-personal conflict have gained followings who are sufficiently partisan to turn the situation into an inter-group conflict. A similar situation can arise from the frustrated leadership aspirations of individuals within the organization.

An organizational conflict may be a genuinely discrete event with an identifiable starting point. More often the origins of conflicts are less easy to identify; they may be symptomatic of longstanding tension within the organization which has gradually built up until the conflict becomes overt. In such situations the stated cause may be no more than the incidental precipitating factor – a convenient label to cover an accumulation of stresses the origins of which may be lost in the history of the organization.

100

Organizational conflict can only be understood in its total context: the internal and external environments of the enterprise; the power relationships characteristic of the enterprise; the goals and frustrations of the groups and individuals concerned. For such reasons it is coming to be accepted that analysis confined to the economic level is inadequate to explore the factors involved. The sociological and psychological perspectives are also essential.

7
Organizational change

It must be considered that there is nothing more difficult to carry out, nor more doubtful of success, nor more dangerous to handle, than to initiate a new order of things. For the reformer has enemies in all those who profit by the old order, and only lukewarm defenders in all those who would profit by the new order, this luke-warmness arising partly from fear of their adversaries, who have the laws in their favour; and partly from the incredulity of mankind, who do not truly believe in any-thing new until they have had actual experience of it.

(Machiavelli, N., c.1513, Tr. Ricci, 1952)

Machiavelli's advice to his Prince still applies to anyone contemplating the introduction of change at any level from the small group to the organization. He may feel that he is faced initially with a fundamental inertia or resistance to change enshrined in sayings such as 'Better the devil you know than the devil you don't know'; 'Out of the frying-pan into the fire'; 'Better safe than sorry' etc.

In an organizational setting, those who advocate or actively support change are likely to be a minority. Even when the case for the inevitability or necessity for change is established beyond any reasonable doubt, there is likely to be ambivalence in the attitudes of those concerned, if not either covert or overt resistance. For the majority incipient change is perceived, at best, as an inconvenient disruption of their lives; at worst, as a threat to their security.

Part of the problem lies in the fact that the complexity of the individual's adaptation to change tends to be under-estimated. What is sought when change is introduced is a modification of individual attitudes, both in their cognitive and their affective components, and an actual change in behaviour. The comment of a member of staff in a re-organized office illustrates this point: 'I've followed the arguments and I can accept that this change was necessary, but I don't really like what it has done to the office and I'm not used to it yet; I find myself slipping back into the old system.'

It would be a mistake to assume that a linear relation-ship exists between such factors as dissatisfaction with an existing system, awareness of the need for change and the possibility of effecting it, on the one hand, and readiness to participate in change on the other. The security of the familiar situation, even if less than ideal, and the anxiety over the unknown or uncertain effects of change militate in favour of the status quo. The possibility also exists that, in the course of adapting to the old system, the individual has reached a compromise and accepted group attitudes and patterns of working which he knows to be imperfect and an appropriate target for change. The dissonance in-volved in the view, 'this is the way I have become used to working, but this style of working can be seen as unsatis-factory and in need of change', is both cognitive and affective.

In studies of nurses' attitudes to change (Barton *et al*, 1961; Glen, 1971) it was noted that the frequency of criticism of the existing system and the readiness to accept change were both negatively related to age and seniority;

that is, the older and more senior the nurse, the less she criticized the system and the less ready she was to accept change. There is some suggestion that if dissatisfaction with the system is sufficiently high in the early stages of the individual's career, they are likely to leave the organization during or soon after the completion of training. If they remain within it, however, the tendency to criticize or to accept change reduces as the individual is promoted within the hierarchy. A further factor militating against the acceptance of change is the experience reported by, amongst others, newly qualified nurses and teachers on taking up their first post of being told: 'You can forget those new-fangled ideas you heard about in training; now you can start really learning the job from the people who have been doing it for years.'

The above comments should not be interpreted as suggesting that only the young are able to view change with favour. Most studies in this area, although often suggesting that the longer one has adapted to a situation the less likely it is that change will be welcome, can point to cases of young, ultra-conservative individuals and of elderly innovators. In many situations, however, the more adaptable, younger members of the group can be the catalysts of change if not the prime movers. A further reason for the absence of any clear indication of a direct relationship between age and the tendency to introduce change is the quite simple one that by the time an individual has reached a position of sufficient authority to initiate change in his organization, he is likely to be somewhat senior in age as well as status. This difference is more obvious in an organizational setting than in social-psychological experimentation, as in the former situation the time spans involved in the establishment of influence within the group are generally much longer.

The change process

The introduction of change in an organization is never a simple additive process. Even if the new situation involves the importation of new people, processes and machinery as a complete unit and no formal change in existing units as specified, there will be a disturbance of the social dynamics of the organization. Even if every member of the organization formally involved in the change has been informed, it does not automatically follow that they will perceive the information as adequate in either form or content. There will also be individuals who receive no formal information as they are not regarded as being concerned in the change; it does not follow that they will see themselves as unaffected. Such situations generally arise as a result of attempts to deal with the change situations as a logical, administrative procedure, neglecting such affective factors as anxiety and insecurity.

Differences in emphasis are evident in current advice to managers in change situations. At first sight, the 'adaptive coping cycle' described by Schein (1965:99) seems to under-emphasize the behavioural and social aspects involved in change. The stages identified are:

1. The sensing of internal or external environmental change.
2. The presentation of relevant information about the change to those parts of the organization which can act upon it.
3. The modification of the production or other operational processes of the organization in the light of the information obtained.
4. The stabilization of the change and the management or reduction of any undesired changes which may arise in related systems as an incidental result of the intended change.

5. Exporting the new products etc, which have been developed to meet the originally perceived change in the environment.
6. Obtaining feedback on the results of the change in terms of success in the external environment and the degree of integration in the internal environment.

In his further discussion of adaptive-coping cycle, reasons for possible failure and the conditions for success, the importance of behavioural and social factors is much more evident than in the original statement.

The advice offered by Lupton (1971:115) to managers concerned in change situations bears very directly upon behavioural or social variables:

1. Set up systematically and in detail the organizational alternatives open.
2. Map out the present organization as a social system, not forgetting its external links.
3. List the groups affected by each organizational alternative.
4. Examine the issues likely to be raised in each group from the adoption of each alternative.
5. Assess likely reactions on each issue and score for acceptability.
6. Test economic feasibility against social acceptability and adopt the course which offers the most adaptive and least costly balance.
7. Examine the problems this course raised and ask whether existing means of redress of grievance are adequate to cope. If not, take appropriate steps to create such machinery as seems to be required.

The source of change may be external to the organization, due to such factors as alternatives in the economic, financial or social environment within which the organization operates; it may be internal as a result of a decision to alter the goals of the organization or the means by which these goals should be reached. It has been argued that change which is made in response to external pressures, with associated increase in internal tension, is more likely to be accepted. The history of the relationship between the organization and its environment is seen as a crucial aspect in the planning and implementation of change.

The change may be mandatory as a result of legislation or of contractual agreements governing conditions of work; it may be forced upon the organization by the incipient failure of its existing systems creating a situation in which it must either change or cease to exist; it may be voluntary, as a result of policy decisions taken to remedy or improve some aspect of the existing situation.

The failure to appreciate that even the best-intentioned or best-planned change is likely to have some disruptive effects in its initial stages can be costly. Faced with this situation it is not unknown for a management to decide that they have made a mistake and to attempt to reverse the process or to introduce unplanned corrective measures. The result is likely to involve not only a reduction or total loss of the benefits of the change, but a high level of dissatisfaction for all concerned. To introduce change is to seek to replace old patterns of behaviour with new learning; it is not to be expected that the new pattern will be perfect at its first performance or that even the best planning will forecast all the incidental effects.

It might seem from the above comments that no management would introduce change without good reason or the fullest consideration of its possible effects, but one occasionally meets the situation in which successive changes have been introduced with such frequency that it becomes almost impossible to separate their effects. In some instances there seems to be a hope that some new technique (insufficiently understood) may solve their problems (inadequately specified); in others there seems to be an organizational variation of 'keeping up with the Joneses' in trying each new procedure as it is developed. 'We tried Management by Objectives last year; that didn't go too well. We're working with Job Enrichment at the moment. Do you think T-groups are a good idea?'

Implementation of change

Change agents are frequently regarded as the key figures in the organizational change process. Buchanan (1967), Leavitt (1965) and Bennis (1966) have all noted the importance of this role in a variety of studies, not infrequently assuming that it is an essential part of any innovative procedure. The term is employed in different ways, usually referring to some form of intervention from outside the organization but sometimes applied generally to those who facilitate the change, sometimes to experts in a consultative role and sometimes to experts in a directive role.

Change agents are seen as introducing a level of detachment and impartiality, as compared to members of the organization who are likely to be too involved in the problem situation to make objective judgements; and also as having some form of expert knowledge relevant to the change situation. The benefits of objectivity and sophistication are undeniable and there are certainly many situations when it is valuable for an organization to call upon outside assistance which can offer skills and experience not available within its own management. The existence of such experts, however, does not relieve management of the responsibility for at least attempting to solve its own problems and introducing procedures to deal with them.

It is not unknown for a management which gives detailed and critical consideration to any proposed expenditure on technological innovation to spend substantial sums on fashionable prescriptions for organizational improvement without adequate evaluation of the problem which they hope to solve or of the suitability of the package which they are buying. Although the outside consultant may be an impartial judge of the organization's problems, it would not be surprising if his advice on possible solutions bore some relationship to the range of expertise which he was able to provide.

Even when the change agent is an academic social scientist, there is the possibility of a certain conflict of interests. On the one hand, he may view the organization as presenting a problem situation calling for investigation; on the other, he may wish to use the organization as a testing ground for the hypothesis with which he is particularly concerned. As we will see, the latter bias can lead to a selective use of the available data or to limitations in the interpretation of findings.

Participation. Here again any review of this topic is complicated by the different usages of the term 'participation'. In general, the term refers to some form of consultation between management and workers (see E5) but it has been applied severally to meetings in which decisions are presented to workers with the opportunity for questions and limited discussion; meetings in which problems may be discussed and suggestions made but where the power of decision remains effectively with management; meetings in which the group may influence the decision process in limited areas or decide between alternative courses of action; and meetings in which there is total participation by the group in a process of planned change.

A further distinction can be drawn between participation in the form of joint consultation as defined by Lupton (1971), and the group of studies in which participation is seen primarily or solely as an approach to increased productivity. The latter aspect could be seen as falling within Lupton's broader definition of joint consultation: 'the formal machinery through which the managers and the workers in a firm, or their elected or appointed representatives, discuss their common problems, decide about them and exchange information'.

The influence of joint consultation and enthusiasm for it has had a rather patchy history in this country since its formal recognition as an industrial practice when it was made a condition of munitions contracts in 1917 during the First World War. Reports of the value of the procedure in different working situations vary from highly successful to complete failure, probably due to the wide variation in interpretation of the practice and to different forms of constraint imposed upon it.

As the different usages of the term 'participation' suggest, the importance of the matters discussed could range in different situations from the crucial to the trivial; not surprisingly, it is difficult to maintain interest in an activity which seems to offer no significant benefits. The reluctance of some managements to allow matters of any importance to be discussed in consultation stemmed jointly from a fear of loss of control and doubts as to the competence and reliability of workers' contributions to what were seen as essentially management problems. Workers' representatives, experienced in bargaining situations, sometimes saw little point in discussing issues which did not appear to have any direct relationship to pay and conditions of work. As this aspect was likely to be excluded specifically from joint consultation procedures by the Employers' Association, the unions, or both, workers in some such situations either lost interest in joint consultation or attempted to use the procedure as an adjunct to conventional bargaining. In either case, the outcome was frequently the end of joint consultation.

When described in broad terms as a generally democratic form of activity, the procedure seems both inherently desirable and relatively straightforward. However, without clear recognition on the part of both management and workers that joint consultation is an approach to the sharing of both power and responsibility, the outcome can be conflict or apathy. Joint consultation conceived of as a relatively painless gesture to democracy is unlikely to be successful.

The outcome, in a particular situation, will be dependent upon the past history of management/worker relations in the organization, the existing climate of relationships in the industry concerned, and the security and social competence of the individuals involved. As a procedure it is both a change situation and a learning situation; it is unlikely, therefore, that the benefits will be immediately apparent. This is borne out by the experiences of long-term studies involving worker participation, whether in the Hawthorne pattern such as the Glacier Metal project (Jacques, 1951 and 1956; Brown, 1960; Brown and Jacques, 1965) or in the field of productivity bargaining such as the Fawley Agreements (Flanders, 1964 and 1967) (see E5).

Participation and productivity. The considerable number of studies carried out in attempts to demonstrate the relationship between employee participation and factors such as morale, commitment to the firm, acceptance of change etc, frequently employ productivity as the indicator of change. Certainly, the majority of the studies indicate that employee participation brings about increased productivity but the relationship is much less clear than some of the advocates of participation suggest.

Argyris (1962) argued that participation was desirable in order to decrease resistance to change, develop the most effective processes for lasting change within the organization, and represent more adequately the needs of the participants involved in the change. He states:

The Coch and French studies and the Morse and Reimer studies are excellent examples of this approach. In the case of the former it was found that the experience

111

of being allowed to participate in decisions usually reserved for management ... increased the workers' effectiveness. In the latter, it was found that high control from above tended to reduce the effectiveness of work groups.

The actual content of the studies in question and the results obtained are rather more complex than this statement would indicate. Morse and Reimer (1956) studied the performance of work groups in an insurance company under two types of supervision, highly directive and structural in one case and democratic and participative in the other. Employee satisfaction, as measured by questionnaire responses, increased under participative leadership and decreased under directive leadership. Productivity, as measured by a cost index, increased under both systems and rather more under directive leadership. The duration of the study was not long enough to show that either result constituted a lasting change within the organization.

The study by Coch and French (1948) is possibly one of the most frequently quoted in this area. New production methods were presented to female pyjama makers: in the control group by simple direction, in one experimental group in consultation with two elected representatives, and in a further two experimental groups with total group participation in the decisions related to the change. Productivity in the two participation groups increased considerably and to some extent in the represented group; in the control group productivity was below the level obtaining prior to the change. Although the main finding is clearly of importance, the overall form of the study is less than satisfactory: the assignment of subjects to groups was not random, the statistical techniques employed were not well-suited to the numbers involved; relevant variables were left uncontrolled and testable assumptions, such as the respective attitudes of the control and experimental groups towards change, were not tested (see A8). The results of a replication study in a Norwegian factory by French *et al* (1960) were much less definite. Another study by Bavelas, quoted in French (1950) showed that operatives who were able to participate in setting production goals showed a significant increase in productivity over control subjects where there was no participation. It should be noted, however, that as the experimental groups received detailed feed-back of results and the control groups had no feed-back, it cannot be proved whether the improvement in control group productivity was due to participation or to feed-back.

The dangers of attempting to manipulate a particular aspect of work behaviour without regard to its total organizational context are well illustrated in a study by Strauss reported in Whyte (1955). Female workers on the painting line in a toy factory were allowed to control the speed of their conveyor belt at will. Although the speed varied during the day, the increase in productivity was considerable. The overall result, however, was something less than beneficial; the supply of materials to the painting line could not be maintained, the production from the painting line could not be used fast enough and piled up; the increased productivity led to earnings out of keeping with those of other workers. The control of the line speed was put back under the control of the management to restore the situation with the result that 75 per cent of the paint-line workers left.

In short, worker participation is not simply an additional incentive situation which can be employed to improve performance, even if it appears to operate effectively in this way on occasion. As a form of social intervention in the dynamics of the organization, it can have beneficial effects on the entire organizational system when it is carefully introduced as part of a programme of planned change on a time span sufficiently long to demonstrate its full effects. As an unplanned intervention it can be disruptive and, if introduced in a situation of existing stress and dissatisfaction, it can precipitate conflict rather than resolve it. As with most organizational innovations, its benefits are most evident when it is designed to meet the unique needs of the setting in which it is employed.

8
Diagnosis and development

With the exceptions of some models and theories, most of which have their origins in Weberian sociology, by far the greater part of the work mentioned in previous chapters has been drawn from the field of applied, as opposed to pure, psychology and sociology. This is not to suggest that field studies have been chosen in preference to laboratory experiments. As Hyman (1964) points out:

> The advantages of observation made under naturalistic methods and in field experiments is that they are obviously relevant to real-life behavior. Yet, this illusion of relevance or actual relevance may be obtained at the cost of vagueness, ambiguity and imprecision. The results of such observations may be suggestive, but they rarely are conclusive because too many factors must be left uncontrolled. One way out of this box is to parallel, wherever possible, field experiments with laboratory experiments.

This 'way out of the box' is open, however, only in so far as the conditions crucial to the study can be replicated in the laboratory (see A8, A9). If, as has been suggested, an event must be understood in its organizational context, a wide range of problems in the social psychology of organizations can only be studied in the field. The extent to which the conditions of the working organization can be manipulated or controlled by the researcher is necessarily limited, even with the maximum degree of co-operation from the management and workers of the organization concerned. Attempts to deal with aspects of this problem are found in the development of 'unobtrusive measures' allowing data to be collected without the awareness of the respondent (Webb *et al*, 1965), a procedure which raises massive ethical problems (see F8). Campbell (1969) has indicated further possibilities of control employing what he terms quasi-experimental design in his treatment of reforms as experiments.

The situation is further complicated by the fact that access to organizations for research purposes is most likely to be granted when some direct benefit to the management concerned is a probable outcome. Consequently, although the primary aims of research in this field should be to understand the social dynamics of organizations, access is more readily granted with a view to correcting some apparent malfunction within the organization or to producing improvement in some aspect of its functioning. In so far as research in an organization sets out to test specific hypotheses it is probable that they will be designed to bring about uni-directional outcomes, i.e. this intervention will increase productivity or reduce absenteeism etc; as opposed to: this intervention will produce a change in the behaviour of the workers, either increased productivity or a strike.

Faced with the fact that access to the organization is likely to be constrained by the expectations of the management concerned, it is necessary to consider some of the difficulties which may arise. In many organizational problems the factors involved are too complex for there to be any reasonable prospect of laboratory replication or of establishing satisfactorily controlled conditions in the field. Such considerations impose limitations on the procedures which may be employed and should also impose a need for caution in the interpretation of results obtained in imperfectly controlled situations.

The identification of problems

The remark attributed to Osler, to the effect that it is more important to understand what kind of patient has a disease than what kind of disease a patient has, could well be applied to organizational research. The parallel is valid in several respects; it can be difficult to judge whether a particular event in a patient or organization constitutes a departure from 'normal' if one does not know what 'normal' is in that situation; some patients/organizations appear to have a much higher capacity to tolerate conflict than others, such differences could lead to the same event being perceived very differently in different situations – a quite usual occurrence in one case, a significant symptom in another.

Although the metaphor is capable of further extension, only two more points require to be stressed: The first is the fact that an understanding of the existing resources and limitations of a patient/organization is necessary if estimates are to be made of the probable effects of a particular kind of malfunction, or of a particular form of treatment. The final clinical comment is to note the relevance, both to people and to organizations, of the distinction between an acute and a chronic condition: the former is sudden of onset and usually sufficiently uncomfortable to attract attention, the latter develops slowly and, in many cases, the organism gradually adapts to the changes and becomes so accustomed to the situation as to be hardly aware that anything is wrong.

The latter point introduces a further complication in the

area of problem identification; the spokesman of the organization is likely to present his statement of the problem and to expect a form of intervention designed on the basis of his statement. The possibility always exists however that what is stated as the presenting problem is, at best, only a part of a more complex situation; the statement offered might even be a mere symptom of an underlying problem of which the organization is not yet aware.

The clinician does not ask the patient what disease he is suffering from; he makes his differential diagnosis on the basis of the history of the case, the presenting symptoms and whatever checks or tests may be available to elucidate the problem. A parallel approach is suggested as appropriate in organizational diagnosis, but it should be remembered that the parallel has limits. The patient rarely argues with the doctor over the diagnosis; on occasion the manager, who feels that he is a good judge of his own organization, may well argue. This is most likely to arise in situations where the organization seeks an intervention to improve its level of performance and the organizational analyst sees the need to correct a basic malfunction before any innovation to bring about improvement is considered.

Effective action is dependent upon accurate diagnosis. Only when the true nature of the problem is, as far as possible, understood will it be possible to make the best judgement of the method of inquiry or forms of intervention required, the extent of change required, the amount of effort likely to be involved and the degree of associated disruption.

In recent years considerable dis-service has been done to the cause of social research in organizations by researchers whose approach has been dominated by the desire to obtain data, or to test hypotheses with little or no consideration for the effects of their activities upon the organization outside the limits of their inquiry. The remains of a biological experiment can be incinerated when the work is completed; volunteer subjects can be thanked and sent away; the organization has to live with the effects of the intervention after the researchers have left.

Organizations which have suffered this type of approach are, not surprisingly, reluctant to repeat the experience, and may well take a rather jaundiced view of the benefits of applied social research. The role of the consultant and problems of organizational diagnosis have been explored in detail by Schein (1969) and Argyris (1970).

Development

Awareness of the importance of social factors in work settings and in the behaviour of organizations has increased steadily during the past half-century. Since the time of the Hawthorne investigation (see E5) the value of the social sciences in both explanation and application has become increasingly apparent in studies of work attitudes and performance, training, conflict and change.

The technique of action research has come to be one of the major tools in organization studies, but concern over some of its application is seen in Rapoport's (1970) suggestion that action researchers have tended to give precedence to action goals rather than to those of research. The original description of the procedure by Lewin (1946) made it clear that two kinds of goal were involved – 'the study of general laws', and the 'diagnosis of a specific situation'. It has been suggested above that the laboratory of the organizational researcher must be the organization itself; on that basis, to neglect the need for theory development through concentration on the solution of specific problems is to retard the development of the subject area. The observation that method, in itself, is no adequate basis for theory development is hardly new:

nothing will be developed by the experimental method except the ideas submitted to it. The method itself gives

119

birth to nothing. . . . If we experimented without a pre-conceived idea, we should move at random, but, on the other hand, . . . if we observed within preconceived ideas, we should make bad observations and should risk taking our mental conceptions for reality. (Bernard, 1865)

The worst types of study seem to be guilty of both forms of error: of inadequate experimental design where the data gathered is inappropriate or insufficient to elucidate the issues involved, and of situations where observations which do not fit the investigator's preconceptions are ignored. Individual solutions and generalized prescriptions are not substitutes for sound theory.

Job design, enlargement and enrichment

During the 1950s developments took place which indicated that approaches derived, on the one hand from the traditions of 'scientific management', and on the other from the 'human relations school', were beginning to find a small extent of common ground. At the risk of over-simplification it might be suggested that one group was beginning to rediscover the relevance of human factors, and the other the relevance of technology.

Ergonomics, the study of design problems at the man/machine interface (see E4), has been described as being derived from engineering, work study, anthropometry, anatomy and physiology and psychology, with the aim of fitting the job to the man (Clay and Walley, 1965). The psychological component, however, often concentrates upon the psychophysiological aspects of the situation, and the traditions of 'scientific management' are often recognizable – as in the title of the work just cited: *Performance and Profitability*. The extension of the concept of job design to take account of the personal, social and organizational aspects of the situation stems mainly from the Berkeley studies described by Davis (1966).

Job enlargement

The rationale of job enlargement (see E5) is developed from similar sources. This approach should involve more than the simple addition of further jobs at the same level – horizontal job loading – by giving the worker a feeling of being responsible for a whole task rather than simply for a step in a process. The procedure also provides for greater variety in work, increased discretion in methods of work and greater responsibility for quality.

In reviews of the results of job enlargement, Aldferer (1969) concluded that it brought about increased job satisfaction and greater meaningfulness of work – he also attributed the mixture of positive and negative effects on interpersonal relations in different studies to differences in technologies. Lawler (1969) found that all of the ten studies which he reviewed reported improvement in quality, but only four showed increased productivity.

Job enrichment

The origin of this approach lies in the studies of Herzberg *et al* (1959) in the field of individual motivation and work (see E5). The emphasis here is upon vertical job-loading – combining a number of hierarchically related functions into a single, more responsible, function. The intention is to provide the worker with opportunities for psychological growth by increased challenge, responsibility and achievement. Reviews of the effects of the job enrichment approach, e.g. Maher (1971), suggest that labour turnover and absenteeism are reduced, job satisfaction is increased, and motivation – often rather loosely defined – is enhanced. Once again it is suggested that the quality of work is improved rather than productivity (Lawler, 1969). This topic suffers from the fact that the design and control of job enrichment interventions is often poor, due to the fact that they have been introduced primarily as prescriptions for improved performance.

121

Some unresolved problems

Evidence is accumulating to call in question the implicit assumption that job enlargement and job enrichment bring about beneficial results for all employees and for all forms of technology. Turner and Lawrence (1968) noted that the effects of increased satisfaction and reduced absenteeism following job enrichment were apparent for small-town workers but not for those in urban settings. Studies by Blood and Hulin, e.g. Blood and Hulin (1969), made broadly similar observations, attributing the findings to the traditional work-values held by non-urban workers as opposed to the alienation of the urban, blue-collar workers.

A further type of finding which questions the generality of the enlargement/enrichment approaches, and also the explanatory value of alienation, is seen in the work of Wanous (1973), who showed that the level of individual needs for accomplishment, variety, challenge etc accounted more effectively for differences in response than did the preceding explanations. Standing (1973) also found a positive relationship between the level of satisfaction in a range of jobs and the cognitive complexity of the employee.

An additional complication in the interpretation of research in this area is the fact that there are significant differences between technologies in the convenience, expense and even the feasibility of implementing job enlargement or job enrichment. In general, although this field of research is clearly important and interventions on this basis can bring about positive results, the variables involved are still imperfectly understood. Greater care and sophistication in research design and a fuller appreciation of the range of differences in technologies, organizational structures and individuals is required before the effects of studies of this type can be fully evaluated.

Group processes in development

The possibility of applying the findings of social psychology and related areas to the problems of team building in organizations has attracted increasing attention in recent years. Although, in a number of cases, enthusiasm to try out new techniques has led to interventions on uncertain theoretical bases, some interesting results have been obtained. French and Bell (1973) describe various approaches to team building.

Comparison and evaluation of the lines of development in this area present problems. These are due, on the one hand, to the combination in the same study of several different methods, and, on the other, to the fact that several of the studies are prescriptive and consequently designed to show the benefits of particular methods rather than to carry out impartial evaluation. Goal-setting discussions, group problem-solving, role analysis studies, 'managerial-grid' approaches to group development and interpersonal relations training have all been employed in the general context of team building (see Blake *et al*, 1964).

In their review of empirical studies of training effects, Campbell *et al* (1970: 287–326) concluded that, although significant effects had been demonstrated and there had been some contribution to knowledge, 'the problem is much more complex than the efforts to attack it to date would seem to imply'. Their comments applied to management development studies up to the end of the 1960s, but there is little evidence of additional clarification in more recent work.

The observations of Argyris (1965), that training in 'interpersonal competence' affected subsequent meeting behaviour in executives, are supported by later studies such as that of Friedlander (1968) who noted that trained groups reported enhanced levels of group effectiveness, mutual influence, personal involvement and participation. The same study, however, found substantial differences between the effects of T-group training (see B1) in different groups, due not to the characteristics of the training experience itself but to the context in which it took place. Evidence on the extent to which the training group experience influences behaviour outside the particular group which has shared the experience is still conflicting.

Although some of the group interventions in organization development amount to little more than the teaching of techniques, others are potentially powerful tools. In particular, the activities variously described as T(-raining) groups, interpersonal development groups, sensitivity training etc (see B1), which trace their origins both to the original work of Lewin and to group psychotherapy procedures, can have profound effects upon the individual if not always upon the organization (see B2). The distinction between 'interpersonal development' and psychotherapy is easier to maintain in theory than in practice and there have been instances of damage as well as benefit to the individual, due to lack of adequate training of group leaders and to inappropriate selection of the group. The leader should have the competence to deal appropriately not only with superficial insights into interpersonal and group dynamics but with unforeseen problems which can arise in this type of situation. The limited depth and duration of the T-group makes it an inappropriate situation for the individual in real need of psychological treatment; personality problems and vulnerable defences can readily be exposed in a T-group, but to do this without a therapeutic goal in view is likely to be damaging rather than beneficial.

On a much larger scale, the work of the Tavistock Institute of Human Relations is producing important developments in the integration of social research with organizational planning and development. An account of their long-term collaboration with the employee relations group of Shell UK Ltd is given by Hill (1971). In the field of industrial democracy the same group are involved

124

in extensive research and field studies in Norway which have important implications for theory as well as practice in the organizational field (Emery and Thorsund, 1969; Thorsund, 1969).

Concluding comments

During the past fifty years many approaches to the understanding of organizational behaviour have been advanced, ranging from theoretical models to prescriptive statements on how to be a successful manager. The backgrounds of the contributors have been correspondingly wide, from researchers in the behavioural and social sciences, some of whom have never worked in anything other than an academic context, to practising managers, some of whom have no formal knowledge of the academic disciplines involved. Not surprisingly, the result has been a somewhat diffuse body of theory, opinions and observations, all too frequently emphasizing the gulf between the theory builders and the practitioners.

In this situation the problem of effective communication is crucial, both to enable the researcher to appreciate the differences between laboratory and field research and to allow the practising manager to see the relevance of research findings to the needs of his organization. Many potentially important hypotheses in organizational behaviour can only be tested in a real-life setting and, as few organizations feel any fundamental obligation to serve the needs of science in this area, access is likely to be given or withheld on a basis of the probable costs and benefits in relation to the organization's goals. The proposals of the researcher must be seen by the practitioner to have relevance to the real problems of his organization as he perceives them.

This introduction to the field of the social psychology of organizations has touched upon topics from the individual level to that of society. Some of the material has been drawn from academic psychology and sociology and some from case studies of actual organizations, with the intention of establishing links between the theoretical basis of the disciplines involved and the complexity of the events which arise in field situations. We are dealing with a series of over-lapping contexts as mentioned above – individual, group, organizational and environmental. To ignore the interrelationships of these levels would be to impose artificial simplification upon the situations.

We are concerned with individuals; the needs, resources and limitations which influence their behaviour and their relations with the organizations to which they belong. We also need to consider the social relationships which develop between people; the influence of the group upon its members and the part which groups play, both formally and informally, in the activities of organizations. The structure of organizations, the technologies involved, the social and economic environments in which they exist, must all be taken into account. These areas are not discrete sub-divisions of the field to be regarded as independent units, but dynamic elements of the internal and external contexts of all organizations.

It has been suggested that both the similarities and the differences between organizations are of importance; although it may sometimes be desirable to simplify a complex area of study by concentrating upon separate aspects, any interpretation of the results obtained must take account of the limitations imposed by this approach, and the need to relate findings to the contexts in which they occur. In strictly practical terms, the credibility of the researcher is not enhanced by the presentation of results which, although significant in terms of the design of the enquiry and the methodology employed, lead to recommendations which are unrealistic and incapable of implementation. This can arise as a result of neglecting human aspects of the problem; for example, a suggested modification of ward organization in a hospital which was rejected because the absolute nature of the senior consultant physician's authority had not been taken into account; and again, potentially beneficial changes in training and staffing in a factory which were not implemented as the conflictful nature of labour/management relations had not been fully appreciated. Other factors can also give rise to problems of implementation; for example, ineffective communication of results, failure to appreciate the nature and extent of financial or technological limitations.

It is suggested that both theory-building and application would benefit from improved communication between researchers and practitioners in all organizational settings and the involvement of the latter, whenever possible, in the design of research and the interpretation of the findings. The specialist skills of the social scientist and the experience of the organizations' members should be seen as complementary resources. Such an approach could be beneficial both in reducing the reserve or even hostility with which the researcher is sometimes regarded and in facilitating the development of our understanding of organizational processes and problems on a basis which is sound both in terms of social science theory and of organizational practice.

For such reasons, and because of the need to examine the interfaces between the individual, group, organizational and environmental levels, no single method of analysis is appropriate to the whole range of problems involved. The approach of social psychology, however, has particular value in this area as it can serve as a link between, on the one hand, the individual and interpersonal aspects of psychology which are essential to the understanding of behaviour in organizations at the micro level, and, on the other, the larger scale social frames of reference of sociology. It also provides a level of analysis which can contribute directly severally to the established theoretical framework of academic social psychology, to the developing area of organization theory, and to the practical problems of application which, although sometimes minimized by the theoretician, are of major concern to the practitioner.

Finally, the approach of social psychology offers model which have the advantages of generating testable hypotheses and also of being readily understood by the members of the organization concerned, who are not only subjects in the research situation but frequently have a direct concern in its outcome. This common interest can form a basis for more effective communication and co-operation in the study of organizations.

Suggested Further Reading

It is probable that there are two main directions from which readers will approach the subject of the social psychology of organizations. The student of psychology, having gained a foundation in the major theoretical and experimental fields of the subject, will be familiar with the bases upon which this area of application rests but may lack experience of actual organizational conditions. The manager or administrator has first-hand experience of work settings but may be less familiar with the general psychological foundations of the subject. These different frames of reference call for differing approaches to background and further reading.

On balance, the main initial need of the psychologist is to gain an understanding of the organizational context in which his subject is applied; that of the manager is to appreciate that a wider understanding of the basic disciplines is of benefit in evaluating the applications of social psychology to his work situation. It is likely that an interested manager will have encountered the ideas of writers such as Argyris, Herzberg, Likert, Douglas MacGregor and Maslow in articles in professional journals and the popular management magazines. If such samples have seemed interesting, there are considerable advantages in reading the author's full statement of his views.

Some texts are suggested below, in addition to the *Essential Psychology* series, which may assist readers in the further exploration of the context of the subject and of specialized topics within it.

General and social psychology

Hilgard, E. R., Atkinson, R. C. and Atkinson, Rita L. (5th edn 1971) *Introduction to Psychology*. New York: Harcourt Brace Jovanovitch.

Wheeler, L., Goodale, R. A. and Deese, J. (1975) *General Psychology*. Boston: Allyn and Bacon.

Hendrick, C. and Jones, R. A. (1972) *The Nature of Theory and Research in Social Psychology*. New York: Academic Press.

Bem, D. J. (1970) *Beliefs, Attitudes and Human Affairs*. Belmont: Brooks-Cole.

Individuals and organizations

Argyris, C. (1964) *Integrating the Individual and the Organization*. New York: Wiley.

Herzberg, F. (1966) *Work and the Nature of Man*. Cleveland: World Publishing.

MacGregor, D. (1960) *The Human Side of the Enterprise*. New York: McGraw-Hill.

Maslow, A. H. (1960) *Motivation and Personality*. New York: McGraw-Hill.

Vroom, V. H. (1964) *Work and Motivation*. New York: Wiley.

Organizations and their problems

Bass, B. M. and Barrett, G. V. (1972) *Man, Work and Organization*. Boston: Allyn and Bacon.

Bennis, W. G. (1969) *Organizational Development: its nature, origins and prospects*. Reading, Mass.: Addison Wesley.

Burns, T. and Stalker, G. M. (1961) *The Management of Innovation*. London: Tavistock.

Lawrence, P. R. and Lorsch, J. W. (1967) *Organization and Environment*. Cambridge, Mass.: Harvard University Press.

Likert, R. (1967) *The Human Organization: its management and value*. New York: McGraw-Hill.

Schein, E. H. (1965) *Organizational Psychology*. Englewood Cliffs: Prentice Hall.

Woodward, Joan (1965) *Industrial Organization: Theory and Practice*. Oxford: Oxford University Press.

References and Name Index

The numbers in italics following each reference refer to page numbers within this book.

Adorno, T. W., Frenkel-Brunswick, Else, Levinson, D. J. and Sanford, R. N. (1950) *The Authoritarian Personality.* New York: Harper and Row. *18*

Aldferer, C. P. (1969) Job enlargement and the organizational context. *Personnel Psychology* 22: 418–26. *121*

Allport, G. W. (1935) Attitudes. In C. Murchison (ed.) *Handbook of Social Psychology.* Worcester, Mass.: Clark University Press. *25*

Anderson, T. and Warkov, S. (1961) Organizational size and functional complexity: a study of administration in hospitals. *American Sociological Review* 26: 23. *80*

Argyris, C. (1960) *Understanding Organizational Behavior.* Homewood: Dorsey Press. *49*

Argyris, C. (1962) *Interpersonal Competence and Organizational Efficiency.* Homewood: Dorsey Press. *11*

Argyris, C. (1965) Explorations in inter-personal competence II. *Journal of Applied Behavioral Science 1*: 255–69. *123*

Argyris, C. (1970) *Intervention Theory and Method.* Reading, Mass.: Addison Wesley. *119*

Asch, S. E. (1952) *Social Psychology.* Englewood Cliffs: Prentice Hall. *29*

Barker Lunn, Joan C. (1970) *Streaming in Primary Schools.*
Slough: National Foundation for Educational Research.
74, 75, 78

Barton, R. (1959) *Institutional Neurosis.* Bristol: John
Wright. *83*

Barton, R., Elkes, A. and Glen, F. J. (1961) Unrestricted
visiting in mental hospitals. *Lancet 1*: 1220–2. *103*

Bennis, W. G. (1966) *Changing Organizations.* New York:
McGraw-Hill. *108*

Bernard, C. (1865) *Introduction à l'étude de la médicine
experimentale.* Paris: J. B. Baillière. *120*

Blake, R. R. and Mouton, Jane S. (1962) The intergroup
dynamics of win-lose conflict and problem-solving collaboration in union-management relations. In M. Sherif
(ed.) *Intergroup Relations and Leadership.* New York:
Wiley. *99*

Blake, R. R., Shepard, H. A. and Mouton, Jane S. (1964)
Managing Intergroup Conflict in Industry. Houston: Gulf
Publishing. *99, 123*

Blau, P. M. and Scott, W. (1968) *Formal Organizations.* San
Francisco: Chandler. *40, 41, 83*

Blood, M. R. and Hulin, C. L. (1969) Alienation, environmental characteristics and worker responses. *Journal of
Applied Psychology 51*: 284–90. *122*

Bray, D. W. and Grant, D. L. (1966) The assessment center
in the measurement of potential for business management.
Psychological Monographs 80: 17 (Whole no. 625). *63*

Brown, W. (1960) *Explorations in Management.* London:
Heinemann. *111*

Brown, W. and Jaques, E. (1965) *The Glacier Project
Papers.* London: Heinemann. *111*

Burt, C. (1969) The mental differences between children. In
C. B. Cox and A. E. Dyson (eds) *Black Paper 2. The Crisis
in Education.* London: The Critical Quarterly Society.

Campbell, D. T. (1969) Reforms as experiments. *American
Psychology 24*: 409–29. *116*

Cane, B. S. and Schroeder, C. (1970) *The Teacher and
Research.* Slough: National Foundation for Educational
Research. *76*

Cartwright, Ann (1964) *Human Relations and Hospital Care.*
London: Routledge and Kegan Paul. *84*

Clay, M. J. and Walley, B. H. (1965) *Performance and
Profitability.* New York: Humanities Press. *120*

133

Cleugh, M. H. (1971) *Discipline and Morale in School and College*. London: Tavistock. *73*

Coch, L. and French, J. R. P. (1948) Overcoming resistance to change. *Human Relations 1*: 512–32. *112*

Cohen, L. (1970) School size and headteachers' bureaucratic role conceptions. *Educational Review 23, i*: 50–8. *79*

Coleman, J. C. (1960) *Personality Dynamics and Effective Behavior*. Chicago: Scott Foresman. *92*

Cronbach, L. G. and Glaser, J. C. (1965) *Psychological Tests and Personnel Decisions*. Urbana: University of Illinois Press. *63*

Dahrendorf, R. (1958) Towards a theory of social conflict. *Journal of Conflict Resolution 2, ii*: 170–83. *93*

Davis, L. E. (1966) The design of jobs. *Industrial Relations 6*: 21–45. *120*

Dollard, J. (1939) *Frustration and Aggression*. New Haven: Yale University Press. *91*

Duane, M. (1968) Incentives and all that. *The European Teacher 6*: 7–20. *73*

Emery, F. E. (1969) *System Thinking*. Harmondsworth: Penguin. *56*

Emery, F. E. and Thorsund, E. (1969) *Form and Content in Industrial Democracy*. London: Tavistock. *125*

Emery, F. E. and Trist, E. L. (1960) Socio-technical systems. *Proceedings, 6th Annual International Meeting of the Institute of Management Sciences*. London: Pergamon. *56*

Emery, F. E. and Twist, E. L. (1965) The causal texture of the organizational environment. *Human Relations 18*: 21–32. *56*

Etzioni, A. (1964) *Modern Organizations*. Englewood Cliffs: Prentice Hall. *36*

Fayol, H. (1949) *General and Industrial Management* (tr. Constance Stores from *Administration Industrielle et Générale*, 1916). London: Pitman. *43*

Festinger, L. (ed.) (1964) *Conflict, Decision and Dissonance*. Stanford: Stanford University Press. *95*

Fiedler, F. E. (1966) The contingency model: a theory of leadership effectiveness. In C. W. Backman and P. R. Secord (eds) *Problems in Social Psychology*. New York: McGraw-Hill. *62*

Fishbein, M. (ed.) (1967) *Readings in Attitude Theory and Measurement*. New York: Wiley. *26*

134

Flanders, A. (1964) *The Fawley Productivity Agreements.* London: Faber. *111*

Flanders, A. (1967) *Collective Bargaining: Prescription for Change.* London: Faber. *111*

Flanders, N. A. (1965) *Teacher Influence, Pupil Attitudes and Achievement.* Washington D.C.: Co-operative Research Monographs no. 12. *75*

Flanders, N. A. (1970) *Analyzing Teacher Behavior.* Reading, Mass.: Addison Wesley. *75*

Ford, J. (1969) *Social Class and the Comprehensive School.* London: Routledge and Kegan Paul. *74*

Forehand, G. A. and Gilmer, B. v. H. (1964) Environmental variations in studies of organizational behavior. *Psychological Bulletin* 62: 361–82. *47, 81, 82*

Fraser, E. D. (1969) *Home Environment and the School.* (Scottish Council for Research in Education, Publication 43). London: University of London Press. *78*

French, J. R. J., Jr (1950) Field experiments: Changing group productivity. In J. G. Miller (ed.) *Experiments in Social Process: A Symposium on Social Psychology.* New York: McGraw-Hill. *113*

French, J. R. P., Jr. and Raven, B. (1959) The bases of social power. In D. Cartwright (ed.) *Studies in Social Power.* Ann Arbor: Institute for Social Research. *38*

French, J. R. P., Jr., Israel, J. and As, D. (1960) An experiment on participation in a Norwegian factory. *Human Relations 13*: 3–19. *113*

French, W. L. and Bell, C. H. (1973) *Organization Development.* Englewood Cliffs: Prentice Hall. *123*

Friedlander, F. (1968) A comparative study of consulting processes and group development. *Journal of Applied Behavioural Science 4*: 377–99. *123*

Georgopoulos, B. S. (1965) Normative structure variables and organizational behavior. *Human Relations 18*: 115–70. *87*

Gilmer, B. v. H. (1971) *Industrial and Organizational Psychology.* New York: McGraw-Hill. *86*

Glaser, B. and Strauss, A. (1968) *The Discovery of Grounded Theory.* London: Weidenfeld and Nicolson. *72*

Glen, F. J. (1971) *Attitudes to change in the hospital service.* Paper presented at Occupational Psychology Section Conference, British Psychological Society, York. *103*

Golembiewski, R. T. (1962) *The Small Group: An Analysis of Research Concepts and Operations.* Chicago: University of Chicago Press. *10*

Hall, R. H. (1963) The concept of bureaucracy: an empirical assessment. *American Journal of Sociology 69, i*: 32–40. *83*

Halpin, C. W. (1966) *Theory and Research in Administration.* London: Macmillan. *76*

Hargreaves, D. H. (1967) *Social Relations in Secondary School.* London: Routledge and Kegan Paul. *74, 75*

Herzberg, F. (1966) *Work and the Nature of Man.* Cleveland: World Publishing. *62*

Herzberg, F., Mausner, B. and Snyderman, B. B. (1959) *The Motivation to Work.* New York: Wiley. *121*

Hill, P. (1971) *Towards a New Philosophy of Management.* New York: Barnes and Noble. *124*

Hovland, C. I. and Weiss, W. (1951) The influence of source credibility on communication effectiveness. *Public Opinion Quarterly 15*: 635–50. *29*

Hoyle, E. (1969) Organization theory and educational administration. In G. Baron and W. Taylor (eds) *Educational Administration and the Social Sciences.* London: Athlone Press. *71, 79*

Hoyle, E. (1973) The study of schools as organizations. In H. J. Butcher and H. B. Pont (eds) *Educational Research in Britain 3.* London: London University Press. *71, 76*

Hyman, R. (1964) *The Nature of Psychological Enquiry.* Englewood Cliffs: Prentice Hall. *115*

Insko, C. A. (1967) *Theories of Attitude Change.* New York: Appleton-Century-Crofts. *26*

Jaques, E. (1951) *The Changing Culture of a Factory.* London: Tavistock. *111*

Jaques, E. (1956) *The Measurement of Responsibility.* London: Tavistock. *111*

Jenkins, G. M. and Youle, P. V. (1971) *Systems Engineering: a unifying approach in industry and society.* London: Wattis. *56*

Jones, Maxwell. (1962) *Social Psychiatry.* Springfield: Charles Thomas. *66, 83*

Kahn, R. L., Wolfe, D. M., Quinn, R. P., Snoeck, J. D. and Rosenthal, R. A. (1964) *Organizational Stress: studies in role conflict and ambiguity.* New York: Wiley. *83*

Kalton, G. (1966) *The Public Schools: a factual survey.* London: Longman. *77*

Kelly, J. (1969) *Organizational Behaviour.* Homewood:

Irwin-Dorsey. *45, 46, 90*

Kelvin, P. (1970) *The Bases of Social Behaviour*. London: Holt Blond. *24, 25, 26, 27*

King, R. (1969) *Values and Involvement in a Grammar School*. London: Routledge and Kegan Paul. *77*

Krech, D., Crutchfield, R. S. and Ballachey, E. L. (1962) *Individual in Society: A Textbook of Social Psychology*. New York: McGraw-Hill. *30*

Lacey, C. (1966) Some sociological concomitants of academic streaming. *British Journal of Sociology 17*: 245-62. *75*

Lambert, R., Milham, S., and Bullock, R. (1970) *A Manual to the Sociology of the School*. London: Weidenfeld and Nicolson. *77*

Lambert, R. with Milham, S. and Bullock, R. (1975) *The Chance of a Lifetime*. London: Weidenfeld and Nicolson. *77*

Lambert, W. W. and Lambert, W. E. (1964) *Social Psychology*. Englewood Cliffs: Prentice Hall. *25*

Lawler, E. E. (1969) Job design and employee motivation. *Personnel Psychology 22*: 426-35. *121*

Leavitt, H. J. (1965) Applied organizational change in industry: structural, technological and humanistic approaches. In J. G. March (ed.) *Handbook of Organizations*. New York: Rand McNally. 1144-70. *108*

Lewin, K. (1946) Action research and minority problems. *Journal of Sociological Issues 2*: 34-46. *119*

Lewin, K. (1965) Group decision and social change. In H. Proshansky and B. Seidenberg (eds) *Basic Studies in Social Psychology*. New York: Holt, Rinehart and Winston. *30*

Likert, R. (1967) *The Human Organization: its management and values*. New York: McGraw-Hill. *53*

Locke, E. A. and Bryan, J. (1968) Goals and incentives as mediators of the effects of monetary incentives on behaviour. *Journal of Applied Psychology 52*: 104-21. *62*

Locke, E. A. and Bryan, J. (1969) The directing function of goals in task performance. *Organizational Behaviour and Human Performance 4*: 35-42. *62*

Lupton, T. (2nd edn 1971) *Management and the Social Sciences*. Harmondsworth: Penguin. *11, 106, 109*

Lutz, F. W. and Iannaccone, L. (1969) *Understanding Educational Organizations*. Columbus: Charles Merrill. *72*

Lynn, R. (1971) Streaming in primary schools. *Educational Research*, Spring. *75*

Machiavelli, N. (*c.* 1513) *The Prince*. Translated Ricci, L., Rev. Vincent, E. R. P. New York: New American Library. *102*

Maher, J. R. (1971) *New Perspectives in Job Enrichment*. New York: Van Nostrand Reinhold. *121*

Mann, R. D. (1959) A review of relations between personality factors and performance in small groups. *Psychological Bulletin* 56: 241–70. *62*

Maslow, A. H. (1954) *Motivation and Personality*. New York: Harper and Row. *62*

Maude, A. (1971) The Egalitarian Threat. In C. B. Cox and A. E. Dyson (eds) *The Black Papers on Education*. London: Davis-Poynter Ltd. *73*

Merton, R. K. (1957) *Social Theory and Social Structure*. New York: Free Press. *91*

Meyer, H. H. (1967) *Differences in organizational climate in outstanding and average sales offices: a summary report.* General Electric, Behavioral Research Service and Public Relations Personnel Service. *87*

Morris, Pauline. (1969) *Put Away: A sociological study of institutions for the mentally retarded*. London: Routledge and Kegan Paul. *83*

Morse, N. and Reimer, E. (1956) The experimental change of a major organizational variable. *Journal of Abnormal and Social Psychology* 52: 120–9. *112*

Munsterberg, H. (1913) *Psychology and Industrial Efficiency*. Boston: Houghton Mifflin. *44*

Musgrove, F. and Taylor, P. H. (1965) Teachers' and parents' conceptions of the teachers' role. *British Journal of Educational Psychology* 35: 171–8. *76*

Newcomb, T. M., Koenig, L. E., Flacks, R. and Warwick, D. P. *Persistence and Change: Bennington College and its students after twenty-five years*. New York: Wiley. *30*

Oppenheim, A. N. (1968) *Questionnaire Design and Attitude Measurement*. London: Heinemann. *26*

Owens, R. G. (1970) *Organizational Behavior in Schools*. Englewood Cliffs: Prentice Hall. *72*

Peaker, G. F. (1967) The Regression Analysis of the National Survey. In *Department of Education and Science. Children and their Primary Schools*. London: HMSO. *78*

Pidgeon, D. A. (1970) *Expectation and Pupil Performance*.

Slough: National Foundation for Educational Research. *75*

Porter, L. W. and Lawler, E. E. (1965) Properties of organizational structure in relation to job attitudes and job behavior. *Psychological Bulletin 64*: 23–51. *81*

Pugh, D. S. (1966) Modern organizational theory: a psychological and sociological study. *Psychological Bulletin 66*: 235–51. *43*

Pugh, D. S., Hickson, D. J. and Hinings, C. R. (2nd edn 1971) *Writers on Organizations*. Harmondsworth: Penguin. *43*

Rapoport, R. N. (1970) Three dilemmas in action research. *Human Relations 23*: 499–513. *119*

Revans, R. W. (1962) Hospital attitudes and communication. *Sociological Review, Monograph 5*: 117. *80*

Revans, R. W. (1965) Involvement in the school. *New Society 6*: 152. *76*

Roby, T. H., Nicol, E. H. and Farrell, F. M. (1963) Group problem solving under two types of executive structure. *Journal of Abnormal and Social Psychology 67*: 530. *82*

Roethlisberger, F. J. and Dickson, W. J. (1939) *Management and the Worker*. Cambridge, Mass.: Harvard University Press. *44*

Rokeach, M. (1968) *Beliefs, Attitudes and Values*. San Francisco: Jossey-Bass. *32*

Rose, G. and Martin, T. F. (1974) *Counselling and School Social Work*. London: Wiley. *76*

Schein, E. H. (1965) *Organizational Psychology*. Englewood Cliffs: Prentice Hall. *34, 63*

Schein, E. H. (1969) *Process Consultation: its role in organization development*. Reading, Mass: Addison-Wesley. *105, 119*

Sherif, M. and Sherif, Carolyn W. (1969) *Social Psychology*. New York: Harper and Row. *22, 26, 28, 30, 86, 95, 98*

Simon, H. A. (1955) Recent Advances in Organization Theory. In S. K. Bailey *et al* (eds) *Research Frontiers in Politics and Government: Brooking Lectures, 1955*. Washington, D.C.: Brookings Institution. *46*

Simon, H. A. (1964) On the concept of organizational goals. *Administrative Science Quarterly 9*: 1. *82*

Sprott, W. J. H. (1958) *Human Groups*. Harmondsworth: Penguin. *10*

Standing, T. E. (1973) Satisfaction with the work itself as a function of cognitive complexity. *Proceedings, 81st Annual*

Convention of the American Psychological Association. 122

Stodgill, R. M. (1950) Leadership, membership and organization. Psychological Bulletin 47 : 1–14. 62

Strauss, A., Schatzman, L., Bucher, R., Ehrlich, D. and Sabshin, M. (1964) Psychiatric Institutions and Ideologies. New York: Free Press. 82

Sykes, A. J. M. (1964) A study in changing the attitudes and stereotypes of industrial workers. Human Relations 17 : 2. 61

Taylor, F. W. (1911) Principles of Scientific Management. New York: Harper and Row. 43

Thompson, D. (1967) Organizations in Action. New York: McGraw-Hill. 60

Thorsund, E. (1969) A strategy for research and social change in industry : a report on the industrial democracy project in Norway. Social Science Information 9, v : 65–90. 125

Titmuss, R. M. (1958) Essays on the Welfare State. London: Allen and Unwin. 84

Trist, E. L. and Bamforth, K. W. (1951) Some social and psychological consequences of the long-wall method of coal-getting. Human Relations 4. 56

Turner, A. N. and Lawrence, P. R. (1968) Industrial Jobs and the Worker. Cambridge, Mass: Harvard University Graduate School of Business Administration. 122

Turner, C. M. (1969) An organizational analysis of a secondary modern school. Sociological Review 17, i : 67–86. 77

Urwick, L. F. (1947) The Elements of Administration. London: Pitman. 43

Urwick, L. F. (1957) Leadership in the Twentieth Century. London: Pitman. 44

Vroom, V. H. (1959) Some personality determinants of the effects of participation. Journal of Abnormal and Social Psychology 59, iii (November). 62

Vroom, V. H. (1964) Work and Motivation. New York: Wiley. 62

Vroom, V. H. (1965) Motivation in Management. New York: American Foundation for Management Research. 62

Wakeford, J. (1969) The Cloistered Elite. London: Macmillan. 77

Wanous, J. P. (1973) Individual differences and employee reaction to job characteristics. Proceedings, 81st Annual

Convention of the American Psychological Association.
122

Webb, E. J., Campbell, D. T., Schwartz, R. D. and Sechrest, L. *Unobtrusive Measures: non-reactive research in the social sciences.* Chicago: Rand McNally. *116*

Weber, M. (1946) *From Max Weber.* (H. H. Gerth and C. W. Mills, eds). London: Oxford University Press. *37, 39*

Whyte, W. F. (1955) *Money and Motivation: an analysis of incentives in industry.* New York: Harper and Row.

Woodward, Joan (ed.) (1965) *Industrial Organization: theory and practice.* New York: Oxford University Press. *44, 45*

Woodward, Joan (ed.) (1970) *Industrial Organization: Behavior and Control.* New York: Oxford University Press. *55*

Wragg, E. C. (1970) Interaction analysis as a feed-back system for student teachers. *Education for Teaching 81*: 38–47. *75*

Subject Index

142

143